Rwanda:

Malaria Operational Plan FY 2014

TABLE OF CONTENTS

ABBREVIATIONS and ACRONYMS

ACT	artemisinin-based combination therapy
ANC	antenatal clinic
AL	artemether-lumefantrine
ASM	*Agents de Santé Maternelle* (specialized maternal community health workers)
BCC	behavior change communications
CCM	community case management
CDC	U.S. Centers for Disease Control and Prevention
CHD	Community Health Desk
CHW	community health worker
DfID	Department for International Development
DHS	Demographic and Health Survey
EIR	entomologic inoculation rate
ESR	epidemic surveillance and response
FANC	focused antenatal care
FHP	Family Health Project
FY	fiscal year
FBO	faith-based organization
GHI	Global Health Initiative
Global Fund	Global Fund to Fight AIDS, TB, and Malaria
GOR	Government of Rwanda
GPIRM	Global Plan for Insecticide Resistance Management
HBMF	home-based management of fever
HCC	Health Communication Center
HMIS	health management information system
ICCM	integrated community case management
IDSR	Integrated Disease Surveillance and Response
IMCI	integrated management of childhood illnesses
IPTp	intermittent preventive treatment of malaria in pregnancy
IRS	indoor residual spraying
ITN	insecticide-treated bed net
IVM	integrated vector management
LLIN	long-lasting insecticidal net
LMIS	logistics management information system
MCH	maternal and child health
MDG	Millennium Development Goals
MIP	malaria in pregnancy
MIS	Malaria Indicator Survey
MOH	Ministry of Health
MOP	malaria operational plan
MPDD	Medical Procurement and Distribution Division
MSP	Malaria Strategic Plan
NMCP	National Malaria Control Program (called the Malaria and Other Parasitic Diseases Division in Rwanda)

NGO	non-governmental organization
NRL	National Reference Laboratory
PEPFAR	President's Emergency Plan for AIDS Relief
PMI	President's Malaria Initiative
QA/QC	quality assurance/quality control
RBM	Roll Back Malaria
RDT	rapid diagnostic test
SIS-COM	community information system
SP	sulfadoxine-pyrimethamine
UNICEF	United Nations Children's Fund
USAID	U. S. Agency for International Development
USG	United States Government
WHO	World Health Organization

EXECUTIVE SUMMARY

Malaria prevention and control is a major foreign assistance objective of the U.S. Government (USG). In May 2009, President Barack Obama announced the Global Health Initiative (GHI), a multi-year, comprehensive effort to reduce the burden of disease and promote healthy communities and families around the world. Through GHI, the United States will help partner countries improve health outcomes, with a particular focus on improving the health of women, newborns, and children. Rwanda has been selected as a GHI Plus country.

The President's Malaria Initiative (PMI) is a core component of the GHI. PMI was launched in June 2005 as a 5-year, $1.2 billion initiative to rapidly scale up malaria prevention and treatment interventions and reduce malaria-related mortality by 50% in 15 high-burden countries in sub-Saharan Africa. With passage of the 2008 Lantos-Hyde Act, funding for PMI was extended through FY 2014. Programming of PMI activities follow the core principles of GHI: encouraging country ownership and investing in country-led plans and health systems; increasing impact and efficiency through strategic coordination and programmatic integration; strengthening and leveraging key partnerships, multilateral organizations, and private contributions; implementing a woman- and girl-centered approach; improving monitoring and evaluation; and promoting research and innovation. Rwanda officially became a PMI country in FY 2007, although the USG had been supporting malaria control activities for several years before that.

Rwanda has scaled up malaria control interventions successfully and has set the ambitious goal of achieving pre-elimination status by 2017. In early 2011, Rwanda was one of the first countries in sub-Saharan Africa to achieve universal long-lasting insecticidal net (LLIN) coverage with the distribution of over 6.1 million LLINs. Rwanda is implementing a universal coverage campaign in 2013 with another national distribution of approximately 6 million LLINs. Rwanda's indoor residual spraying (IRS) has targeted high-burden districts and sectors, based on available evidence. Rwanda has conducted nine IRS rounds to date and has withdrawn IRS operations in certain districts due to reduction in malaria incidence, transmission, and funding. Rwanda currently sprays two rounds annually in three high malaria burden districts that border malaria-endemic neighbors. In 2013, Rwanda developed and is implementing an insecticide resistance management (IRM) plan that builds upon their Integrated Vector Management (IVM) strategy. Rwanda will change the insecticide class it uses in IRS in a phased transition and continue to switch classes every two years based on evidence of insecticide resistance and World Health Organization (WHO) guidance. Progress in case management is equally impressive with great strides in diagnosis and treatment at all levels of the health care system and nationwide integrated community case management. In late 2009, the MOH, through its Malaria and Other Parasitic Diseases Division (termed in this MOP the National Malaria Control Program, or NMCP) directed that all presumed malaria cases be laboratory confirmed. In 2012, HMIS reports indicate that 99% of all patient-diagnosed malaria cases are confirmed by microscopy or rapid diagnostic tests before receiving ACTs. Community health workers (CHWs) continue to play a pivotal role in malaria case management and 30,000 of Rwanda's extensive network of 60,000 CHWs are mobilized to implement integrated community case management (iCCM), diagnosing and treating malaria, diarrhea, and pneumonia.

The results of these efforts are documented in the 2010 Demographic and Health Survey (DHS) and decreasing malaria trends are visible in the health management information system (HMIS). The 2010 DHS reports a net ownership rate of 82% (compared with 57% in the interim DHS of 2007/2008) and net usage rates by children and pregnant women at 70% and 72% (compared with 58% and 62% in 2008), respectively. National household-level malaria prevalence estimates in children under five continue to decline, from 3% in 2007/2008 to 1.4% in 2010. Malaria control efforts, combined with significant improvements in maternal and child health, vaccinations, and HIV/AIDS, have reduced all-cause under-five mortality by 50%, from 152 deaths per 1,000 live births in 2005 to 76 deaths per 1,000 live births in 2010. From 2006 to 2011, the Rwandan HMIS has shown remarkable improvements in malaria indicators: an 86% reduction in malaria incidence, 87% reduction in malaria morbidity, 74% reduction in malaria mortality, and a 71% reduction in malaria test positivity rate. However, Rwanda has been experiencing an upsurge of reported cases in 2012 and 2013. Indeed, compared to 2011 levels, reported cases have more than doubled in 2012.

The FY2014 Malaria Operational Plan for Rwanda was developed in consultation with the NMCP and with the participation of all national and international partners involved in malaria prevention and control in the country. The activities that PMI is proposing to support with FY 2014 funding align with the vision of the draft 2013-2017 National Malaria Strategy to achieve pre-elimination by 2017 and will build on investments made by PMI and other partners to improve and expand malaria-related services with an emphasis toward enhanced surveillance, monitoring and evaluation. The proposed FY 2014 PMI budget for Rwanda is $18 million. Based on Government of Rwanda (GoR) malaria control gap analyses in the Malaria Strategic Plan (MSP), discussions and meetings with the NMCP and partners, the following major activities will be supported:

Indoor residual spraying (IRS): PMI supports the NMCP's strategy to reduce malaria transmission through IRS in targeted high-risk areas. The 2012 spray round protected approximately 1 million residents in three border districts. The coverage rate was more than 98% of the 242,589 targeted structures. The next spray round will take place in September 2013 using a carbamate insecticide and a second round will occur in February 2014. In 2013, in preparation for the phased transition of IRS implementation from the PMI implementing partner to the GOR, PMI, the NMCP, and stakeholders conducted an IRS capacity assessment, where Rwanda showed strengths in leadership, coordination, planning, entomological monitoring, and implementation. Recommendations were provided for improving logistics, environmental compliance, and monitoring and evaluation at decentralized levels, which will improve IRS capacity. With FY 2014 funds, PMI will deploy IRS, with continued emphasis on capacity building in the context of moving IRS support through government-to-government funding. Spraying with FY 2014 funds will mark the second year of transitioning components of IRS activities directly to the GoR, including payment of spray operators, transport, warehousing, training and supervision. In FY 2014, it is envisaged that the GoR will spray three districts. The PMI implementing partner will retain responsibility for procurement of insecticide, technical assistance for supervision, quality control and assurance, and environmental monitoring in all three districts.

Insecticide-treated nets (ITNs): The NMCP achieved universal LLIN coverage, defined as one net for every two people or three nets per household, in February 2011. PMI has been collaborating with the NMCP and Global Fund to maintain universal coverage for all age groups, and a replacement campaign is ongoing in late 2013. The main delivery channels include free mass distribution during integrated health and vaccination campaigns, and routine distribution of free nets through antenatal care (ANC) and Expanded Program for Immunization clinics in all health centers. In 2013 and 2014, PMI has planned to procure 400,000 LLINs to support routine LLIN distribution and 1 million LLINs to maintain universal coverage through a mass campaign. PMI is collaborating with the NMCP to support net care messaging to increase net longevity and will consider LLIN replacement more frequently if recommended by WHO.

With FY2014 funding, PMI will procure 375,000 nets. These nets will be distributed through routine distribution channels targeting pregnant women at ANC and infants in EPI clinics. PMI will also support an assessment to determine if LLIN disposal is a problem or if LLINs are being repurposed appropriately. If issues are noted, PMI will provide technical assistance to develop and implement a disposal strategy. In addition, PMI will continue to support the LLIN distribution systems to district and community levels to prevent stockouts and will increase behavior change communication (BCC) activities at national and community levels, particularly among CHWs, to promote correct and consistent net use.

Malaria in pregnancy (MIP): Because of increasing parasite resistance to sulfadoxine-pyrimethamine and decreasing malaria prevalence, the NMCP discontinued intermittent preventive treatment of malaria in pregnancy (IPTp) in 2008. PMI continues to support other interventions to prevent and promptly detect and treat malaria in pregnant women, including procurement of LLINs and distribution to pregnant women at ANCs, training of health care workers on focused antenatal care (FANC), and support to a cadre of maternal health community health workers (Agents de Santé Maternelle - ASMs) who monitor pregnant women in their village and encourage them to attend their ANC appointments. The Maternal Child Health (MCH) Program, in coordination with the NMCP, the Community Health Program, and the Expanded Program for Immunization, with support from PMI and other partners, has developed an integrated approach to deliver quality health care for pregnant women. The services provided by MCH units, in addition to fetal growth monitoring and birth preparation, make up the focused antenatal care package, which is now available nationwide.

With FY2014 funding, the NMCP, PMI, and partners will continue to support early diagnosis and treatment of MIP and LLIN procurement and distribution to pregnant women. PMI, in coordination with USG MCH programs and the MOH, will also continue to facilitate supervision of MCH-focused CHWs (known as ASMs) by health center supervisors, contribute to their training, evaluate performance of community outreach to pregnant women, and strengthen linkages between ASMs and health facilities to promote LLIN use, ANC attendance, and early detection and treatment of malaria in pregnant women.

Case management: All health facilities officially transitioned to artemether-lumefantrine (AL) as the first-line treatment for uncomplicated malaria in October 2006. In November 2009, the NMCP revised their treatment policy to require diagnostic confirmation of all fever cases. The Global Fund to Fight AIDS, Tuberculosis and Malaria (Global Fund) procured the majority of ACT needs for Rwanda. However, the Global Fund's single stream financing ends in June 2014.

PMI is working with the NMCP and the MoH to apply for the new funding model with the Global Fund.

In line with GHI principles, PMI has helped capacity building and systems for integrated community case management of fever, as well as strengthening laboratory diagnostic training and supportive supervision systems. With FY2014 funding, PMI will continue to strengthen efforts to ensure prompt and effective case management of malaria at health facilities and at the household/community level by CHWs through scale-up of iCCM of malaria, diarrhea, and pneumonia. PMI will procure ACTs and RDTs to help fill gaps in iCCM commodities. PMI has supported the full iCCM package in seven districts and plans a phased transition to government-to-government funding in these districts with FY 2014 funds. PMI will also continue to fund BCC activities to promote timely treatment seeking and proper use of ACTs. At the health facility level, PMI will concentrate on strengthening capacity in laboratory diagnostics and supply chain management. PMI will strengthen quality assurance/quality control (QA/QC) systems at national and district levels for accurate malaria diagnosis, and will support the NMCP's supervisory role to monitor and reinforce the correct use of ACTs at health facilities and in communities.

Monitoring and evaluation (M&E): Both PMI and the President's Emergency Plan for AIDS Relief have contributed to strengthening Rwanda's M&E systems with noticeable improvements. HMIS data are sufficiently complete, accurate, and timely to be used for routine program monitoring. NMCP staff analyze these data, produce maps and charts showing the geographic distribution and trends in malaria cases, and make programmatic decisions based on this data. In September 2012, PMI, in collaboration with WHO and Global Fund, supported the NMCP in organizing and implementing the first Malaria Pre-Elimination Forum, which brought over 50 international experts in malaria control and elimination, as well as neighboring and pre-elimination country NMCP managers, to discuss and provide Rwanda with recommendations on what is needed to achieve pre-elimination by 2017. The recommendations of the forum were included in the draft 2013 – 2017 Malaria Strategic Plan.

With FY2014 funding, PMI will continue to support the NMCP to strengthen evidence-based decision making throughout the health system and strengthen surveillance. The GoR has prioritized decentralization, and with a decreasing malaria burden and a transition from stable to unstable malaria transmission, the ability for districts to analyze and respond to upsurges in malaria is pivotal. Therefore, PMI will support the NMCP in strengthening decentralized M&E capacity. PMI will continue to work with the NMCP to prioritize and build capacity in enhanced passive surveillance and in epidemic surveillance and response in order to build the foundation that Rwanda needs to achieve the ambitious goal of pre-elimination by 2017.

Behavior change communication: With FY2014 funding, PMI will continue to support implementation of Rwanda's national health communication strategy, as well as the national malaria communications strategy. New plans and strategies for BCC will depend on the success of the activities of the communications project begun in 2013, which will focus on six high-prevalence districts, and on the changing malaria situation, both in Rwanda and in neighboring countries. If the situation evolves as expected, with Rwanda ready for pre-elimination by 2017, BCC will focus on risk perception with reminders that malaria can still return, so people should continue to sleep under nets and be sure to go to the health facility or community health worker if anyone has fever. In districts that share borders with other countries, BCC will need to be intensified for residents, in particular those who cross borders into neighboring countries. Efforts aimed at those who enter Rwanda from countries with high malaria transmission should be considered as well. In 2013/2014, PMI will support the updating of the malaria-specific BCC strategic plan, which was in effect through 2012.

Health systems strengthening, capacity building, and transition: As shown by the 2010 DHS results and trends in the HMIS, Rwanda has made a strong commitment to improve the health of its citizens through a wide range of health systems strengthening efforts. Consistent with GHI principles, PMI has contributed to health system strengthening by capacity building at the NMCP through support of seconded staff, continued strengthening of the Health Management Information System, the National Reference Laboratory, and Logistics Management Information System, and the integration of service delivery within other programs, such as MCH and EPI.

As a part of GHI, PMI and the GOR are supporting integrated service delivery, including integration of malaria control with MCH and community-based health service delivery. PMI is supporting the iCCM approach. It partners with the MCH program to ensure children under five years of age have access to treatment of malaria, diarrhea, and pneumonia through CHWs and health facility staff.

In FY 2014, PMI is progressing with the USAID Forward policy of transition and building sustainability through government-to-government funding. The NMCP has proven that it has the capacity to implement malaria control interventions such as iCCM, IRS, nationwide surveillance, and monitoring and evaluation. PMI will coordinate with the NMCP to streamline the transition and provide support in the process.

STRATEGY

Introduction

The President's Malaria Initiative (PMI) is the United States Government's response to malaria prevention and control in sub-Saharan Africa. PMI was launched in June 2005 as a five-year program with funding of $1.2 billion and a goal to reduce malaria-related mortality by 50%. The strategy for achieving this goal was to reach 85% coverage of the most vulnerable groups – children under five years of age and pregnant women – with evidence-based preventive and therapeutic interventions, including artemisinin-based combination therapies (ACTs), insecticide-treated bed nets (ITNs), intermittent preventive treatment during pregnancy (IPTp), and indoor residual spraying (IRS). Owing to PMI's progress, in 2008 the Lantos-Hyde Act extended funding for PMI with the revised goal of a 70% reduction in malaria-related mortality by 2015.

Rwanda was selected as a PMI country in FY 2007. Large-scale implementation of ACTs and LLINs distributions began in 2007 and progressed rapidly with support from PMI and other partners. Since 2006 with the support of the Global Fund, ACTs have been available and are being used in all public health facilities nationwide, and in 2011, Rwanda achieved universal coverage of its population with ITNs (one ITN for every two people).

This FY 2014 PMI Malaria Operational Plan presents a detailed plan for the eighth year of PMI in Rwanda and is based on a joint gap analysis of malaria control in Rwanda developed between the NMCP and relevant malaria control stakeholders. It is also informed by a new (draft) 5-year 2013–2017 National Malaria Strategic Plan (MSP), which is being finalized. The new strategy aims at achieving pre-elimination by 2017. This operational plan briefly reviews the current status of malaria control policies and interventions, describes progress to date, challenges and unmet needs if the national targets of NMCP and PMI are to be achieved, and provides a description of planned FY 2014 activities. The activities that PMI is proposing to support with FY 2014 funds are aligned with the 2013-2017 MSP and build on investments made by PMI and other partners (including the Global Fund to the single-stream funding mechanism) to expand malaria-related services. The total amount of PMI funding requested in FY 2014 for Rwanda is $18 million.

Country Malaria Situation

Rwanda is a small, land-locked country in the Great Lakes region of eastern Africa, bordered by Uganda, Burundi, the Democratic Republic of the Congo, and Tanzania. It has a population of approximately 10.8 million (projections based on the 2012 census results), making it the most densely populated country in continental Africa. Administratively, the country is made up of 30 districts, which are divided into sectors, cells "cellules," and 14,953 "umudugudus" (villages of 50-100 households). The entire population is at risk for malaria, including an estimated 2.2 million children under five and 443,000 pregnant women/year (projections based on the 2012 census results).

The country is divided into four malaria ecologic zones based on altitude, climate, level of transmission, and disease vector prevalence (Figure 1). Malaria is mesoendemic in the plains and prone to epidemics in the high plateaus and hills. The Malaria and Other Parasitic Diseases Division (NMCP) in Rwanda has classified 19 (63%) of the country's 30 districts as epidemic-prone and the remaining 11 as endemic. Malaria transmission occurs year-round with two peaks (May-June, November-December) in the endemic zones following distinct rainy seasons. In addition to climate and altitude, other factors that influence malaria in the country include high human concentration (e.g., boarding schools in proximity to marshlands); population movement (especially from areas of low to high transmission); irrigation schemes (especially in the eastern and southern parts of the country); and cross-border movement of people (especially in the eastern and southeastern parts of the country).

Figure 1. Rwanda elevation, health centers, boundaries, and malaria risk stratification

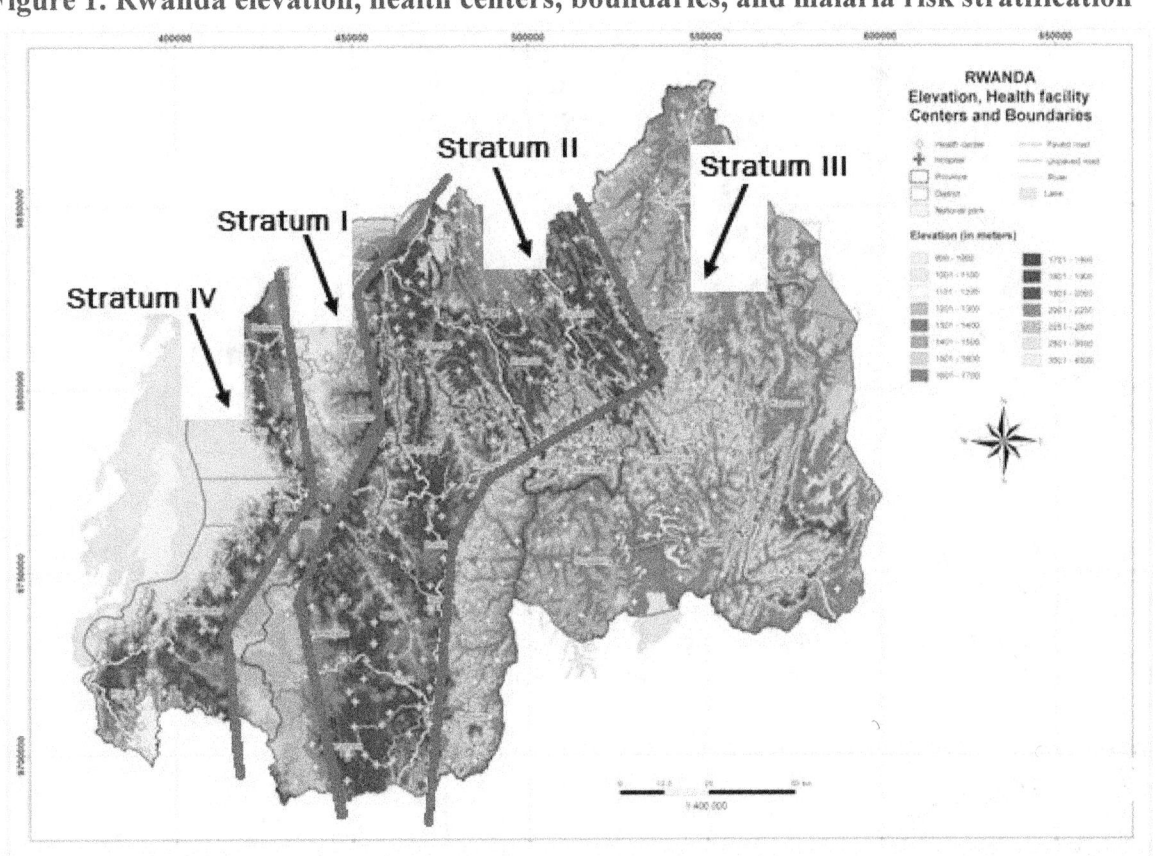

Country Health Delivery System and MoH Organization

The Rwanda Health System has five tiers and is led by the MOH (Figure 2). The MoH supports, coordinates, and regulates all interventions whose primary objective is to improve the health of the population. The mission statement of the MoH is "to provide leadership of the health sector to ensure universal access to affordable preventive, curative and rehabilitative health services of the highest attainable quality."

Figure 2. Rwanda health system

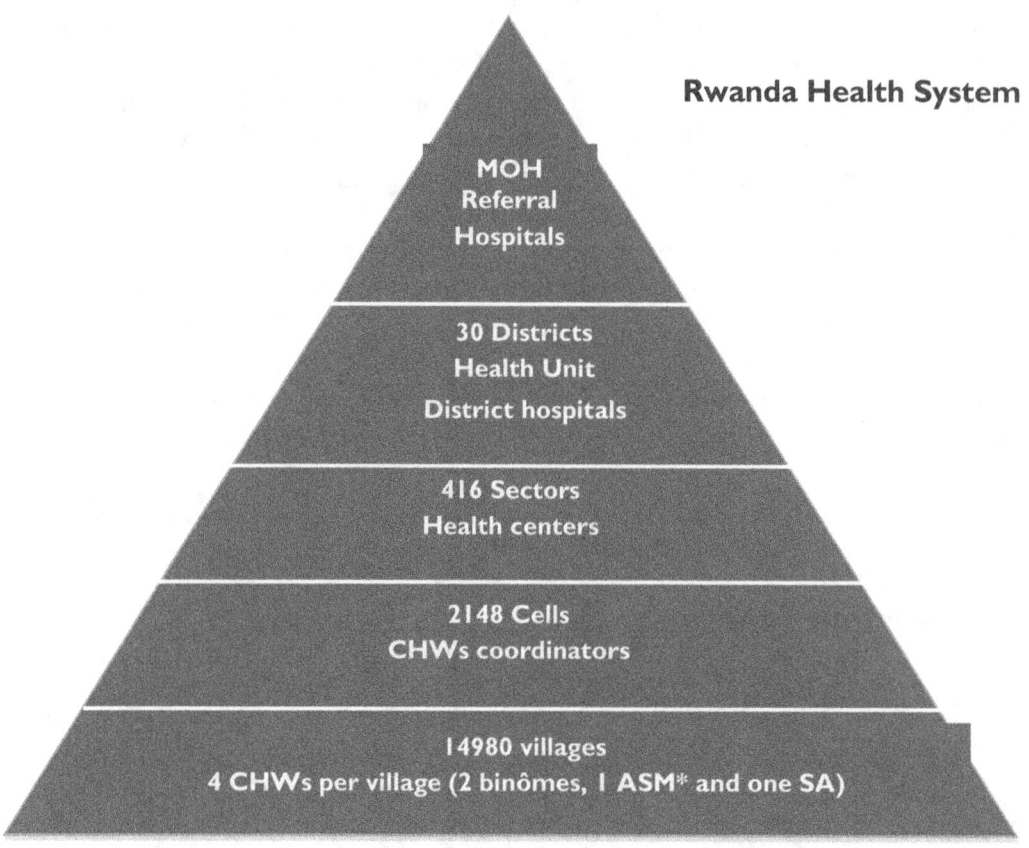

CHW = community health worker; binome = two community health workers (male and female) in a village who implement iCCM; ASM = Agent de santé maternelle; SA = social affairs community worker

Services are provided at different levels of the health care system (community health, health posts, health centers, district hospitals and referral hospitals) and by different types of providers (public, faith-based, private-for-profit and nongovernmental organizations).

Health Facilities

Public health facilities represent 55% of the total number of health facilities in Rwanda; an additional 22% are run by faith-based organizations, 20% by private organizations, 2% by communities, and 1% by parastatal organizations.

The number of public health facilities in Rwanda at the end of 2012 was 720, up from 579 in 2010. This increase was primarily due to the opening of 80 new health posts, 60 new dispensaries, and 6 health centers. In the tables and figures below, these facilities are classified as referral hospitals, district hospitals, health centers, dispensaries, and health posts (Figure 3).

Figure 3. Distribution of health facilities by type, 2012

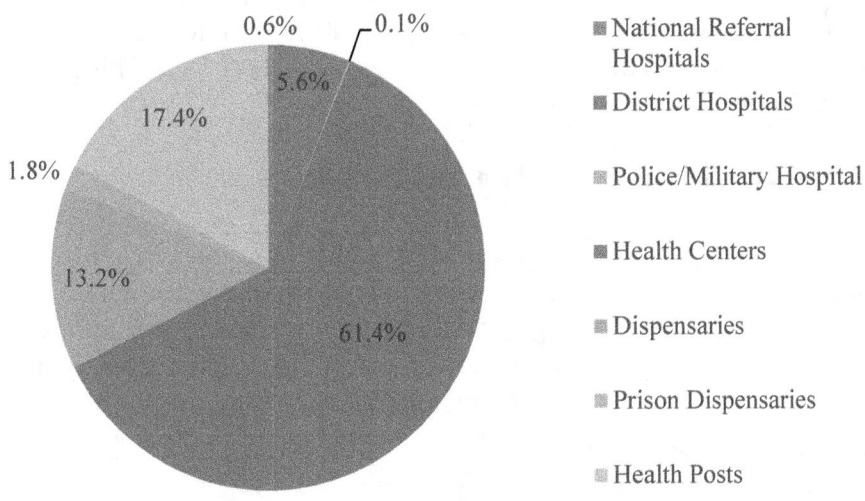

- National Referral Hospitals
- District Hospitals
- Police/Military Hospital
- Health Centers
- Dispensaries
- Prison Dispensaries
- Health Posts

Source: Health Facilities Database, HMIS Unit, 2009-2011

Figure 4. Geographical distribution of health facilities per district, 2011

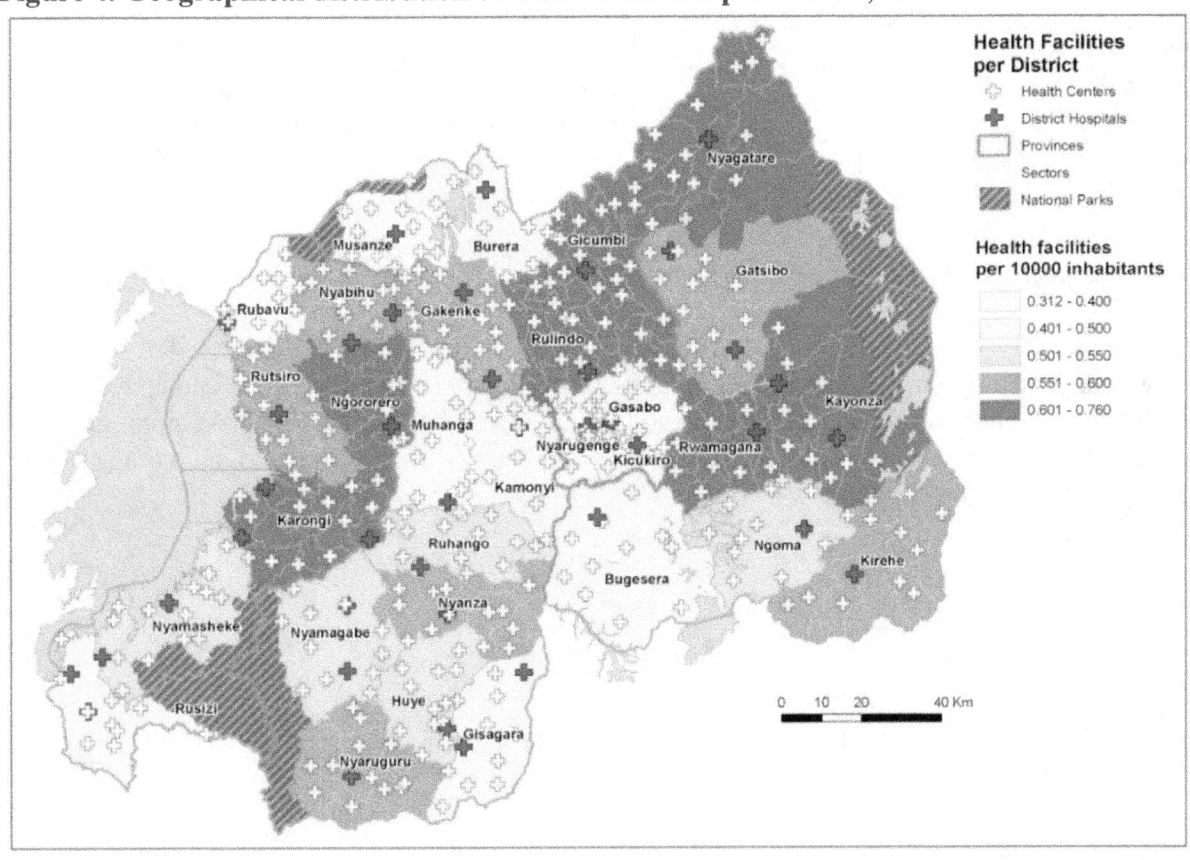

Referral System

An extensive network of public sector health centers exists to meet the health needs of Rwanda's population. This network is structured as a pyramid with three referral hospitals at the apex supported by 42 district hospitals and 524 health centers (Figure 4). The health centers, in turn, use a network of 60,000 community health workers (CHWs) and other community-based associations for community outreach activities. Referral hospitals also serve as teaching institutions for doctors and pharmacists.

Minimum package of services in different types of health facilities

Health Facilities	Minimum Package of Services Provided
National Referral Hospital	Advanced inpatient/outpatient services, surgery, laboratory, gynecology, obstetrics, and radiology; specialized services including ophthalmology, dermatology, ear nose and throat, stomatology, and physiotherapy
District Hospitals	Inpatient/outpatient services, surgery, laboratory, gynecology obstetrics, and Radiology
Health Centers	Prevention activities, primary health care, inpatient, referral, and Maternity
Dispensaries	Primary health care, outpatient, and referral
Health Posts	Outreach activities (i.e., immunization, family planning, growth monitoring, ANC)

All health centers and facilities above that level have at least one functional microscope and reagents needed for the diagnosis of malaria. The referral system is anchored by the provision of an average of four ambulances per district as well as the CHWs' access to cell phones.

Administratively, Rwanda consists of four provinces and Kigali City, 30 districts, 416 sectors, 2,148 cells, and 14,980 villages. The 2010 DHS showed that 78% of the households have at least one family member with health insurance and that among those insured 98% have community health insurance (*mutuelles*). Each district has at least one district hospital and an average of one health center per 20,000 people.

National Malaria Control Plan and Strategy

The NMCP, in collaboration with Roll Back Malaria (RBM), WHO, Global Fund, PMI, and partners, is currently finalizing a new 2013–2017 Malaria Strategic Plan (MSP). It addresses challenges and gaps identified in a Malaria Program Review, which was completed in March 2011, and incorporates recommendations from a malaria pre-elimination forum that took place in September 2012 as well as the two gap analysis workshops carried out by the NMCP in collaboration with all stakeholders. The strategy's goals and objectives are aligned with three of the Government of Rwanda's primary strategic documents: Vision 2020, the overarching strategy used to guide long-term development in Rwanda; Economic Development and Poverty Reduction Strategy for 2013–2018; and Rwanda's mid-term development plan, which in turn serves as the framework for the national Health Sector Strategic Plan III for 2012–2018. See graphic below.

NSP, National Strategic Plan
HSS, Health System Strengthening

With the significant reduction in malaria cases over the past 10 years, the GoR/NMCP articulated an ambitious vision of a Rwanda free from malaria as a way to contribute to socio-economic development. It has targeted a new goal to achieve pre-elimination nationwide by 2017, by reducing malaria morbidity to pre-elimination levels of less than 5% test positivity rate among febrile patients and by lowering mortality by 50% from the 2011 baseline level. This goal is elucidated in the draft 5-year 2013–2017 MSP, which provides distinct objectives, addresses gaps observed in the implementation of Rwanda's previous strategies, and provides detailed approaches to achieving malaria-related results and targets. This strategy aims to sustain progress, to scale up the most effective malaria control and prevention activities from the health facility to the community level, and to involve all partners (including the private sector) in supporting health care delivery in Rwanda.

Under the 2013–2017 MSP, the NMCP assumes the lead coordination role and takes responsibility for the decentralization of malaria control and prevention activities throughout the country. The NMCP coordinates the contributions of all health partners, donors, and private sector stakeholders.

The NMCP sets the following objectives to reach by 2017:
- Ensure that 95% of the population has correct knowledge of malaria prevention and treatment.
- Reduce the number of cases of severe malaria by 70% from the 2011 level.
- Strengthen national and international partnerships, including cross-border malaria control initiatives aimed at harmonization and coordination of interventions.
- Treat 95% of malaria cases in accordance with the national malaria treatment guidelines.
- Ensure that 90% of the population at risk is effectively protected by at least one appropriate preventive measure.
- Control 100% of malaria epidemics within 2 weeks following their onset.

Strategic Interventions of the draft 2013-2017 Malaria Strategic Plan

Integrated Vector Management (IVM)

Following a vector control needs assessment conducted in 2010 and the Malaria Program Review in 2011, Rwanda adopted an IVM strategy in 2013 that provides a comprehensive framework for vector control interventions. In particular, it guides selection of vector control options and optimal application of these interventions based on knowledge of local vector ecology, disease epidemiology, and socio-economic and operational factors. The use of LLINs nationwide and IRS in three high-burden districts remain the cornerstone vector control methods featured in the IVM strategy. In 2012, the NMCP in collaboration with PMI and other stakeholders, developed and implemented an insecticide resistance management (IRM) strategy, which was adopted in 2013, based upon WHO's Global Plan for Insecticide Resistance Management (GPIRM), which prioritizes protecting the efficacy of the LLINs by mitigating emerging resistance to pyrethroids. Officially adopted in February 2013, the IRM strategy calls for a phased transition from pyrethroids to carbamates and subsequently to long-acting organophosphates if this is approved for public health use.

Achievement and maintenance of universal coverage of LLINs

Rwanda achieved universal LLIN coverage, defined as one net per two people, in February 2011 with the distribution of 6.1 million bed nets during rolling campaigns from 2010 to early 2011. The NMCP intends to maintain universal coverage levels by developing a long-term LLIN procurement and distribution plan to:
- Ensure a continuous supply of replacement nets
- Identify additional targeted populations and new delivery channels
- Sustain financing to ensure the predictability and availability of resources
- Establish country-specific net replacement and disposal guidelines

- Monitor the lifespan of insecticide efficacy and net durability
- Strengthen procurement mechanisms to avoid delays
- Monitor and report on net use quarterly through community health volunteers.

Preliminary results from a longitudinal three-year LLIN field study of net durability suggest a shorter duration than recommended by manufacturers and that there is a need for enhanced net care to prolong durability. There will also be on-going BCC efforts to sustain high LLIN use.

Evidence-based focused IRS

The IVM strategy supports targeted IRS based on malaria burden as measured by health facility epidemiological case data and entomological parameters. Nine spray rounds with a pyrethroid have been conducted with PMI support since 2007. Data from 2011 on insecticide resistance from 14 sentinel sites across the country showed high vector susceptibility to pyrethroids (99% mosquito mortality for lambdacyhalothrin and 97% for deltamethrin), delayed knock-down, and high prevalence of knock-down resistance gene (*kdr*), which indicated that resistance to pyrethroids might be emerging. In 2012, NMCP data on insecticide resistance from five sentinel sites indicated an established resistance to pyrethroids (deltamethrin and lambdacyhalothrin) and waning efficacy of carbamates (84% efficacy) in one sentinel site in Nyagatare. This study is currently being repeated for confirmation. These findings were instrumental in the development and adoption of the IRM strategy described above (under IVM).

Malaria in Pregnancy

Most pregnant women attending antenatal care (ANC) in Rwanda receive two of the three recommended MIP control interventions for medium and high transmission settings. First, an LLIN is provided to women in their first pregnancy during their first visit to an ANC clinic. Second, pregnant women with fever are tested for malaria by microscopy and then treated if positive. Rwanda discontinued IPTp in 2008 based on evidence of the high therapeutic failure of SP in 6- to 59-month-old children and a study which found no added benefit of IPTp with SP compared to placebo with regard to maternal hemoglobin, newborn weight, and placental parasitemia; and decreasing malaria prevalence nationwide.
Maternal mortality in Rwanda fell from 750 deaths (2005 DHS) to 476 deaths (2010 DHS) per 100,000 live births, a 36% decline. Most (98%) pregnant women visit an ANC at least once (although the median gestational age at first visit is late at six months), and 35% of women make four or more ANC visits. Net usage among pregnant women rose from 17% (2005 DHS) to 62% (2007/2008 interim DHS) to 72% (2010 DHS). The MOH Maternal Child Health (MCH) Desk has coordinated with NMCP, the Community Health Desk (CHD), and Expanded Program on Immunization (EPI) to strengthen integration of ANC services. The services provided by these units, in addition to fetal growth monitoring and birth preparation, make up the focused antenatal care (FANC) package, which is now available nationwide. Specialized community health workers (*Agents de Santé Maternelle* [ASM]) focus specifically on women in communities, including pregnant women and their newborns, and are included in the malaria in pregnancy strategy. The ASMs identify pregnant women early, distribute a first dose of low-dose iron, folic acid, and mebendazole for anemia prevention, and promote LLIN use and early and regular (up to four) ANC visits. Early ANC attendance is also encouraged by providing targeted BCC,

combined with innovative community- and facility-level performance-based financing and high enrollment in community health insurance schemes (*mutuelles*).

Case Management

Malaria diagnosis

In July 2009, Rwanda's National Malaria Treatment Policy mandated that all cases of suspected malaria should be laboratory confirmed prior to treatment with an ACT. The policy applies to all age groups and health facilities, iCCM, and the private sector. The infrastructure for malaria diagnosis has improved in the past few years, all health facilities currently have a functioning microscope and at least one laboratory technician and according to the HMIS, 99% of the malaria cases were parasitologically confirmed at health facilities in 2012. The draft National Strategic Plan stresses the need to strengthen capacity for differential diagnosis including detection of low-level parasitemia at health facilities and at the community level.

As part of the expansion of iCCM, training in RDT use for CHWs and health center supervisors, including laboratory technicians, was conducted in all districts. The NMCP, in collaboration with WHO, CHD/MoH, and NRL is organizing the validation of RDTs based on the technical specification elaborated with partners including PMI. These criteria include a panel detection rate >80% for *P. falciparum* at 200 parasites per μl, as well as a false positivity rate and an invalid rate both below 3%.

Malaria treatment at health facilities

In October 2006, all health facilities officially transitioned from amodiaquine-SP to artemether-lumefantrine (AL) as the first-line treatment for uncomplicated malaria. Treatments are provided at a highly subsidized price at health facilities. Oral quinine is the second-line treatment for cases of uncomplicated malaria and when AL is contraindicated. For patients who cannot tolerate oral medications, the national guidelines recommend the use of injectable artemether or intravenous quinine until the patient can take oral medications. Health centers refer cases of severe malaria for treatment to district hospitals or referral hospitals. In 2010, Rwanda participated in an 11-country, open label, randomized trial whose findings showed that artesunate substantially reduces mortality in African children with severe malaria. These data, together with a meta-analysis of all trials comparing artesunate and quinine, strongly suggest that parenteral artesunate should replace quinine as the treatment of choice for severe *P. falciparum* malaria worldwide. With these results, the NMCP in 2011 adopted parenteral artesunate in place of quinine as the first-line treatment for severe malaria. PMI procured the first consignment of 40,000 vials of parenteral artesunate in 2012 and will procure another 62,000 vials in FY 2013. The NMCP has conducted cascade trainings in all districts with the support of the Global Fund on this treatment policy, and its implementation was officially launched on June 1st 2013.

Provider acceptance of the diagnostic policy change is reflected in an increasing number of blood smears performed and a declining number of presumed malaria cases treated and reported since the policy was enforced, according to HMIS data.

Malaria treatment in the community

The draft 2013-2017 MSP regards the integrated community case management of malaria (iCCM) and other diseases not only as a strength, but also as an opportunity for leveraging other health programs' funds. Building on the home-based management of fever model, the MOH CHD has introduced and consolidated iCCM to include malaria, pneumonia, diarrhea, and other components (nutrition, family planning, hygiene, and palliative care). The iCCM package is being implemented by 30,000 CHWs nationwide. Training of CHWs, first offered in July 2009, including training in use of cell phones for data reporting, is now conducted annually. PMI and the Global Fund have supported the expansion through CHW training, provision of materials (e.g., CHW kits, registries, job aids), supervision, and monitoring. All districts have introduced RDTs into the iCCM package and have now transitioned to the full iCCM package as outlined in the revised Community Health Strategy.

Malaria treatment in the private sector

From 2008 through most of 2010, the GOR supported treatment of children under five in private sector pharmacies and over-the-counter outlets (*comptoirs*), by subsidizing ACTs. In 2010, the NMCP suspended provision of the subsidized ACTs, which had been repackaged and co-branded with the name *"PRIMO"* before sales, because of new malaria treatment guidelines, which mandated diagnostic confirmation before provision of ACTs. According to the national pharmaceutical regulations, RDTs and blood smears cannot be made available at private pharmacies or drug outlets.

A 2009 study showed private sector usage of less than ten percent in major cities, but beyond that, there is little known about nationwide access of the private sector for malaria treatment or antimalarial-dispensing practices of private providers.

Drug supply and pharmaceutical management

The MOH procures antimalarials and supplies for health facilities through the Medical Procurement and Distribution Division (MPDD), part of the Rwanda Biomedical Center. The MPDD currently procures about 60% of all facility drugs and supplies and is the only institution in Rwanda that can legally procure ACTs for the public sector. With support from President's Emergency Plan for AIDS Relief (PEPFAR), USAID family planning programs, and the Global Fund, MPDD has undergone fiduciary risk assessments and has qualified as a USG direct funding recipient pending negotiation of risk mitigation strategies with the GOR. PEPFAR is planning to move antiretroviral (ART) procurement to MPDD in the FY 2013 country operation plan; PMI will not transition procurement of commodities to the MPDD in FY 2014. However, USAID and PMI will continue to support capacity building within the MPDD and will consider transition if the MPDD ART procurement is successful and all assessments and risk mitigation strategies are completed.

In 2013, malaria commodities will be integrated into the coordinated procurement and distribution system (CPDS) with family planning, HIV, and other health commodities, which improved donor coordination and flexibility with responding to delivery delays or other impediments. PMI, Global Fund, and other stakeholders have also participated in malaria gap analyses and malaria commodity technical specification workshops to ensure there were no gaps in malaria commodity availability.

A paper-based Logistics Management Information System (LMIS) for all program-related commodities was launched in 2011, and an electronic LMIS system (e-LMIS) will be implemented in 2013, funded by PMI and the Global Fund. The LMIS harmonized the process for collecting logistics data across all programs. A joint PMI and PEPFAR assessment of the supply chain was conducted in August of 2011 to evaluate the implementation of the LMIS and measure system performance including product availability at the facility and district pharmacy levels for a variety of products.

With PMI and PEPFAR funds, USAID is assisting with the establishment and training of the Logistics Management Office (LMO). LMO is in charge of all the logistics data entry, aggregation, and analysis used to make policy decisions and to aid in decision making during forecasting and quantification. The LMO also provides supportive supervision of supply chain management to health facilities and district pharmacies. New directors have been named and capacity building has been prioritized by the MoH in the context of transition and the possibility of government-to-government financing.

Parliament approved the creation of the Rwanda Food and Medicines Regulatory Authority in 2013. The authority will assist the Pharmacy Task Force in implementing its mandate to guarantee quality control of incoming and circulating drugs. The Pharmacy Task Force was created in 2005 to oversee retailers and serve as the national drug regulatory authority. Its responsibilities include conducting quality control, inspection, and licensure, and ensuring a basic package of pharmaceutical products. The NMCP conducts antimalarial drug quality control annually with the support of the pharmacy department of National University of Rwanda, where drugs collected at all levels of health care are sampled and sent for drug analysis.

Monitoring and Evaluation

The epidemiology of malaria in Rwanda is shifting, as evidenced by remarkable reductions in outpatient malaria cases measured by the HMIS and drastic declines in parasitemia and anemia in children under five measured by household surveys (DHS and MIS). Although overall Rwanda is still in the malaria control phase, 19 out of 30 districts (63%) have been reporting slide positivity rates less than 5% among febrile patients, which is the WHO threshold for programmatic transition to a malaria pre-elimination phase. Pre-elimination requires increased attention in ensuring good-quality surveillance data by mandating that suspected malaria cases receive a diagnostic test, cases are correctly classified according to the test result, a quality management system exists for both microscopy and RDTs, and registration and reporting from health facilities are complete and consistent.

The following information sources guide MOH's programmatic decision-making:

- *HMIS*: The HMIS indicators and forms were revised and a new web-based platform (DHIS2), with geospatial information system capacity, was launched in 2010. The HMIS receives data from all public health facilities, with timely and accurate reporting reinforced through performance-based financing. As of late 2010, the system provided data on only laboratory-confirmed malaria outpatient cases, inpatient cases, and deaths, as well as data by age and gender on all-cause morbidity and mortality at individual facilities. Since 2012, the community information system SIS-COM has been linked to HMIS through DHIS2. Private sector treatments are currently not reported.

- *Community information system:* This system originally included two systems: a paper-based system with performance-based financing, through which CHWs linked to the HMIS by reporting to the nearest health facility and a cell phone–based system that sends data directly from CHWs to the CHD. The system was transitioned into the community-based SIS-COM (*mUbmizima*), which includes community diagnosis, treatment, and essential drug logistic information. SIS-COM is separate from the HMIS, although since 2012, it has been linked to the HMIS through the DHIS2 web-based platform. SIS-COM incorporates a real time, web-based data platform, with a minimum set of indicators. The registers and reporting formats were designed specifically to collect community data generated by CHWs using cell phones. As of November 2012, all 30 districts were trained on the cell phone–based reporting system.

- *Integrated Disease Surveillance and Response (IDSR):* Surveillance activities are coordinated and streamlined throughout all levels of the health system from the community, health facility, district hospital and central levels. The MOH has conducted a surveillance assessment and is in the process of updating the current IDSR as well as computerizing the reporting and monitoring system. Cell phone–based reporting is also being piloted for IDSR. There is a functional weekly epidemiological reporting system in place.

- *Entomological surveillance:* See Vector Control/Entomology Section.

- *Logistics management information system (LMIS):* A paper-based system harmonized across all programs launched in early 2011 provides basic data on drug consumption, lab commodities, and stock outs at health facilities, independent of the HMIS. Reports flow from health facilities to district offices to MPDD and will be used for quantification. Currently, data are provided by the HMIS and district pharmacy reports to the MAL & OPP through biannual quantification workshops with all district pharmacy directors. An automated LMIS will be rolled out in 2013, which will improve data quality and access.

- *DHS/MIS:* These comprehensive nationwide household surveys provide a broad range of population-based data, including bed net indicators (ownership and use by vulnerable populations), and malaria parasitemia and anemia. Population-based indicators change rapidly in Rwanda; thus, the GOR repeats surveys every two years. A full DHS was completed in 2010, and an MIS was conducted in 2013, with the final report expected by late 2013. The current MIS includes malaria-related behavioral questions but does not include biomarkers, but the upcoming 2014/2015 DHS will collect malaria and anemia biomarkers.

- *Research and routine monitoring activities:* Activities include participating in household surveys to track use of LLINs, monitoring drug and insecticide efficacy, evaluating community case management, participating in health facility surveys, and malaria in pregnancy.

Rwanda has a costed Monitoring and Evaluation (M&E) Plan, which includes the disease integration effort being promoted by the MOH. However, the Malaria Program Review identified some challenges, including limited data on malaria-related socio-economic impact and no data reporting from private clinics and national referral hospitals. The action points suggested to address the challenges were partially or completely implemented during 2012, including the strengthening of analysis and use of routine data for action at national level and building key malaria indicators into the HMIS data warehouse and dashboard (where users can view real-time graphs, charts, and maps of malaria, etc). However, incorporating referral hospitals and private clinics into the HMIS remains a challenge.

Behavior Change Communication

Behavior change communication and social mobilization play an important role in the timely and correct use of interventions to diagnose, treat, and prevent malaria. In 2011, Rwanda developed and adopted a national integrated BCC strategy to harmonize the communication activities and messages for health sector interventions, including malaria and other infectious diseases, maternal health, and family planning. The strategy stresses advocacy for leadership and direction and social mobilization with a focus on positive changes in social norms and individual behaviors. These integrated BCC activities include a combination of interpersonal communication, community education and mobilization, information, education and communication, trainings, and media campaigns to influence and/or modify behaviors and environmental factors. These activities will be carried out at the national and community levels.

Now that malaria cases and deaths have fallen so dramatically, it is important that residents in Rwanda are aware of the risks associated with malaria, those with symptoms of malaria are diagnosed and treated, and measures to prevent malaria are taken. Continued priorities include social mobilization around the distribution of new and replacement nets, provider and caregiver acceptance of case management policy, and household acceptance of IRS. Moreover, following the Malaria Program Review, the NMCP refined and shifted some of their BCC priorities. New focuses of BCC research include improving malaria risk perception and increasing use of prevention methods such as LLINs and IRS. The NMCP's specific BCC strategy expired in 2012 and PMI will support the development of a new strategy in FY 2013. PMI Rwanda would also like to measure the effects of BCC programs and use these data to strengthen the BCC strategy.

Integration, Collaboration, and Coordination

In addition to PMI, other development assistance for malaria comes from the Global Fund (Figure 5), RBM and WHO. Rwanda has one active Global Fund malaria grant that has been implemented since July 2011 and will continue until June 2014. The Global Fund grant supports the expansion of community case management with RDTs, antimalarials for treatment at health facilities and in the community, procurement of LLINs, the strengthening of monitoring and evaluation systems, and resources for health communications, HSS, HMIS, and program management operating costs. The NMCP did not apply to the Global Fund's Transitional Funding Mechanism because there were no gaps in the continuation of essential malaria activities or supply of commodities. In 2013, the NMCP applied for the $6-million Global Fund interim funding grant to ensure continuity of operations until the full roll-out of the New Funding Model in 2014.

Figure 5. Global Fund and PMI support to Rwanda, 2006–2012

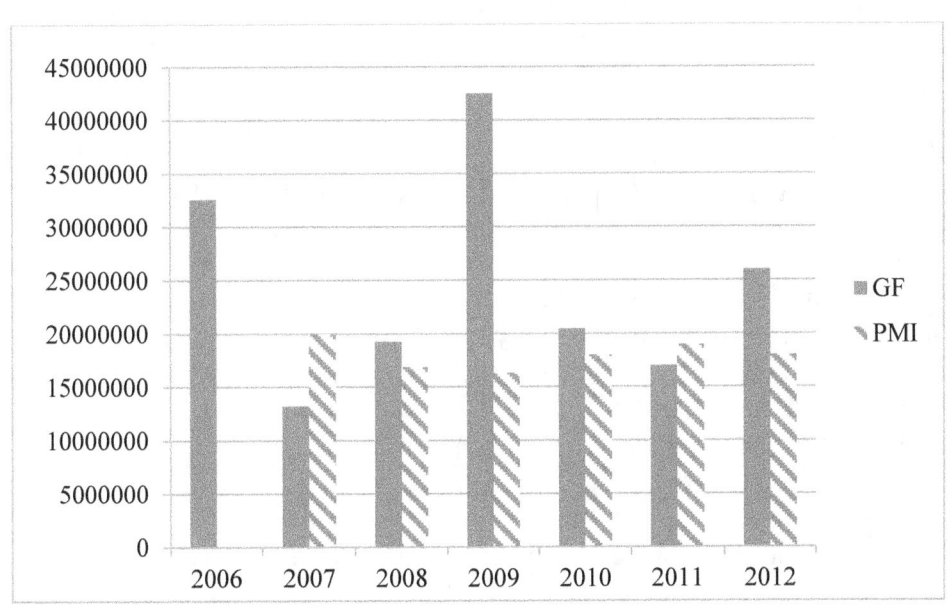

Source: www.theglobalfund.org; www.pmi.gov

Goal and Targets of the President's Malaria Initiative in Rwanda

The goal of PMI is to reduce malaria-associated mortality by 70% in the 15 original PMI countries. By the end of 2015, PMI will assist Rwanda to achieve the following targets in populations at risk for malaria:

- >90% of households with a pregnant woman and/or children under five will own at least one ITN;
- 85% of children under five will have slept under an ITN the previous night;
- 85% of pregnant women will have slept under an ITN the previous night;
- 85% of houses in geographic areas targeted for IRS will have been sprayed;

- 85% of pregnant women and children under five will have slept under an ITN the previous night or in a house that has been sprayed with IRS in the last 6 months;
- 85% of government health facilities have ACTs available for treatment of uncomplicated malaria.

Progress on Indicators to Date

Health Management Information System

The primary sources of information used to track trends in malaria prevalence and coverage indicators are aggregated case reports from health facilities and national household surveys. The HMIS collects monthly data on the number of reported cases (presumed and confirmed) of malaria and deaths attributed to malaria by age group from the over 524 health centers and district hospitals. SIS-COM (community information system) collects data from the community health workers and integrates the data with HMIS. Performance-based financing and monthly data quality audits, showing concordance between clinic registers and HMIS reports, encourage completeness of reporting.

Based on HMIS data, Rwanda has seen an 84% decline in confirmed malaria cases from 1.5 million in 2005 to an unprecedented low of 227,015 in 2011, representing a significant reduction in transmission, even in the context of the change in malaria case definition.

From 2010 to 2011, there was a decline in malaria reported cases, a 45% decline in the number of malaria deaths, and a 5% decrease in the slide positivity rates. However, Rwanda is experiencing an increase in malaria incidence, which is being analyzed by the NMCP and has been documented in all Eastern African countries. The NMCP is currently preparing for a scheduled universal net distribution campaign in July 2013, which will hopefully halt the increasing trend.

The HMIS also collects test positivity rates on an annual and monthly basis. See Table 1 below.

Table 1. Summary of malaria data reported through the Health Management Information System, 2008–2013[1]

	2008	2009	2010	2011	2012
Total cases reported	772,197	1,322,622	663,785	225,176	487,150
% confirmed[1]	41%	51%	94%	99%	99%
% morbidity[2]	11.8%	15.2%	7.8%	3%	5.9%
Test positivity rate[3]	18%	54.3%	24%	13.1%	15.6%
Malaria-attributed mortality[4]	16.3%	19.2%	12.9%	6.4%	6.0%

[1]Proportion of suspect cases that received laboratory confirmation by microscopy or RDT.
[2] Up until 2010, % morbidity relates to % of fever cases with malaria. In 2011, the denominator changed from fever cases to all outpatient cases. It represents confirmed malaria new cases as a percentage of all outpatient new cases).
[3]Test positivity rate: malaria positive tests divided by total tests of suspect cases.
[4]Up until 2010, malaria-attributed mortality in all age groups represented the proportion of deaths attributed to malaria by laboratory confirmation. In 2011 this indicator reflects % of patients admitted for malaria who died, which is the same as *case-fatality rate*.

Figure 6 depicts the increased malaria burden in 2012 compared to 2011, as measured by test positivity rates from health centers throughout the country. Given such high confirmation rates, the NMCP plans to use test positivity rates instead of parasite prevalence to stratify malaria burden by district and to monitor the impact of interventions.

National Household Surveys

Rwanda conducted a full DHS survey in 2005, an interim survey in late 2007/early 2008, and a full DHS survey in 2010. The NMCP also conducted a National Malaria Indicator Survey (MIS) in 2007/2008 and in 2013. These surveys show marked improvements in key prevention indicators, as summarized below. For example, in 2005, 15% of households owned an ITN, and 13% of children under five and 17% of pregnant women had slept under one the night before. The 2010 DHS showed that 82% of households owned at least one ITN, and that 70% of children and 72% of pregnant women had slept under one. It is important to note that 2.5 million LLINs were distributed after the 2010 DHS data collection, and therefore the 2013 MIS was conducted to update LLIN ownership and use rates in Rwanda. These gains in bed net ownership and use parallel the reductions in malaria parasitemia observed in children under five over the same period: from 2.6% in 2007/2008 to 1.4% in the 2010 DHS.

Indicator	DHS 2005	Interim DHS 2007/2008	DHS 2010
Proportion of households with at least one ITN	15%	57%	82%
Proportion of children under five	13%	58%	70%

years old who slept under an ITN the previous night			
Proportion of pregnant women who slept under an ITN the previous night	17%	62%	72%
Malaria prevalence in: Children under five Women of childbearing age	N/A (not available)	2.6% 1.4%	1.4% 0.7%
Under five all-cause mortality (per 1,000 live births)	152	103	76

Sources: Rwanda 2005 DHS; Interim DHS 2007/2008, DHS 2010, possible 2013 MIS (preliminary)

Figure 7, below, shows malaria prevalence data per province. It can be seen that the geographical distribution of the malaria burden follows the same pattern evidenced by the above HMIS TPR data in Table 1.

Figure 7. Household-level parasite prevalence in children under five years of age, by province, 2010

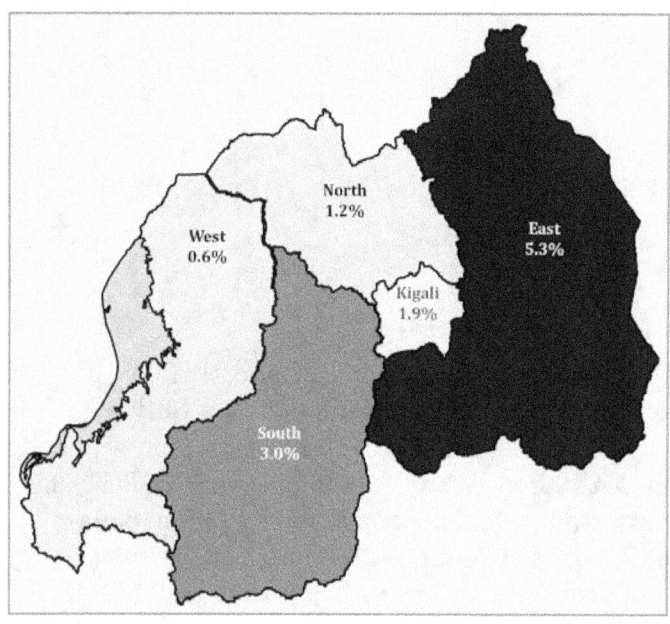

Source: DHS 2010

PMI Support Strategy

The overall PMI strategy for Rwanda is aligned, complementary, and supportive of Rwanda's draft 2013–2017 National Malaria Strategic Plan, whose vision is to achieve pre-elimination status by 2017. To achieve this, strategic investments should be made that leverage resources from the GOR, development partners, and technical agencies.

PMI's national-level support includes health system strengthening, support to the HMIS and SIS-COM, improvement of pharmaceutical and commodity supply chain management, and enhancement of BCC activities. Integrated interventions, including diagnostics, iCCM, MIP, surveillance/monitoring/evaluation, and provision of antimalarial commodities in health facilities and communities, are specific priorities that PMI will continue to support and to gradually transition to the MoH.

Rwanda has prioritized decentralization and PMI will support this effort with building and transitioning capacity and supporting programs in the districts, health centers, and the community. Several USAID funding streams including those for HIV/AIDS, maternal and child health, and family planning will be combined with PMI resources to support this goal.

Expected Results – Year Eight

PMI and the NMCP have agreed on the following outcomes for FY 2014:

Prevention

1. LLINs: Procure and distribute 375,000 LLINs through routine distribution channels to contribute to maintenance of universal coverage.
2. IRS: Support spraying of approximately 250,000 structures in two rounds in targeted districts based on epidemiologic and entomologic data.

Treatment

1. Diagnosis in the community: Procure and fill the existing gap with 1.2 million RDTs and safety boxes to support laboratory diagnostic confirmation prior to treatment through community case management.
2. Community case management: Strengthen community case management of fever (iCCM) integrated into the full community health care package in 7 out of 30 districts.
3. Support for case management at health facility level: Procurement of AL, parenteral artesunate, and lab supplies.
4. Support QA/QC at community level through health facilities and district hospitals.

Surveillance, Monitoring, and Evaluation

1. Enhance decentralized surveillance to generate timely, high-quality, and individual-based data to track, analyze, and respond to malaria trends. This will support malaria pre-elimination activities in 5-10 districts.
2. Epidemic Surveillance and Response (ESR): Continue to strengthen the ESR system by developing new epidemic thresholds and developing standardized operating protocols.
3. Document increases in malaria indicators, reductions in malaria burden both in terms of entomologic and epidemiologic parameters, and measure outcome and impact through surveys.

OPERATIONAL PLAN

Vector Control: Integrated Vector Management (IVM), Indoor Residual Spraying (IRS), and Insecticide-Treated Nets (ITNs)

Integrated Vector Management (IVM)

NMCP/PMI objectives

In response to the need to develop long-term strategies for slowing down and mitigating the selection for vector resistance, the NMCP is reorienting toward an IVM approach that seeks to use evidence to improve the efficacy, cost-effectiveness, and sustainability of vector control. The IVM strategy outlines five key elements in this process: (1) advocacy, social mobilization and regulatory control, (2) collaboration within the health sector and with other sectors to optimize use of resources, planning, and monitoring, (3) integration of vector control measures, (4) evidence-based decision making guided by entomological and epidemiological surveillance and evaluation, and (5) development of human resources and infrastructure at national and local level.

Following a vector control needs assessment in 2010 and the Malaria Program Review in 2011, an IVM strategy was developed to provide a framework that guides decisions on selection of vector control options and optimal application of these options based on local vector ecology, disease epidemiology and other socio-economic and operational conditions. The strategy calls for continued, high-quality entomologic monitoring. The use of LLINs and IRS remain the cornerstone vector control methods featured in the IVM strategy.

Progress during the last 12 months

In 2013, Rwanda's 2012-2016 IVM strategy was adopted during an intersectoral stakeholder meeting. An insecticide resistance management plan for Rwanda (see details in IRS section) was also developed and adopted at a stakeholders meeting held in February 2013. Both documents were brought up for review at the MoH senior management meeting and were signed by the Minister of Health. The process of establishing an intersectoral coordination mechanism and a vector control technical working group is underway.

With PMI and Global Fund support, the NMCP maintained entomologic surveillance across 12 sentinel sites. In 2011, insecticide susceptibility studies were conducted in an additional 2 sites, bringing the total to 14 sites. At the time, data from non-IRS and IRS areas indicated warning signs of possible emerging resistance to some pyrethroid compounds, full susceptibility to bendiocarb and fentrothion, and resistance to DDT in some areas. In 2012, the NMCP conducted another insecticide susceptibility study in five sites which showed established resistance to pyrethroids in Mimuri, a sentinel site in Nyagatare.

Figure 8. Insecticide resistance testing in 5 sentinel sites, Rwanda 2012

Sites	Organochlorine	Carbamates	Organophosphates	Pyrethroids	
	DDT 4%	Bendiocarb0.1%	Fenitrothion 1.0%	Deltamethrin 0.5%	Lambdacyhalothrin 0.75%
Mimuli (Nyagatare)	84%	84%	100%	23%	20%
Kivumu (Rutsisro)	100%	99%	100%	100%	97%
Rwaza (Musanze)	99%	100%	100%	99%	98%
Mubuga (Karongi)	97%	98%	100%	97%	90%
Mareba (Bugesera)	97%	100%	100%	90%	86%

In 2013 PMI supported the refurbishment of an insectary (an integrated vector control laboratory) that is expected to be handed over to the NMCP in September 2013. In addition, three staff members from the NMCP were sent to KEMRI and ICIPE, Kenya, for training in polymerase chain reaction (PCR) techniques on mosquito identification and KDR analysis. This included training on safe management of an insectary.

The NMCP also conducted mosquito species identification via PCR, in Kenya on selected samples from 6 sites. Results indicated a high predominance of *Anopheles arabiensis* among malaria vectors and a high prevalence of the *kdr* gene among *A. gambiae s.l.*, which may explain the now established resistance to pyrethroids in one district.

Challenges, opportunities, and threats

Rwanda was one of the first African countries to adopt an IVM strategy, and key stakeholders–such as the Ministry of Agriculture, Ministry of Natural Resources, and other MOH departments–have been eager to collaborate. However, there is lack of experience in implementation of IVM in stable malaria transmission settings in Africa.

Gap analysis for vector control needs: IVM

The IVM strategy seeks to leverage existing community-based platforms for its implementation, which may decrease implementation costs. The Global Fund has been supporting implementation, and many of IVM's entomologic monitoring needs are covered elsewhere, and thus a gap analysis is not included in this section.

Entomologic Monitoring

PMI and Global Fund support data collection and analysis of five primary indicators: malaria vector taxonomy and density, malaria vector distribution and seasonality, malaria vector insecticide susceptibility/ mechanisms of resistance, malaria vector biting time and location, and LLIN and IRS insecticidal effect at 12 sites.

Plans and justification

PMI will continue to support routine entomologic monitoring, which will be transitioned entirely to the NMCP through the government-to-government mechanism.

Proposed activities with FY 2014 funding ($370,000)

- Support the full entomologic monitoring package in 12 sentinel sites, including equipment (dissecting microscopes), an entomology technician, and training for the new insectary, susceptibility testing, bioassays for IRS quality control and efficacy, and determination of resistance mechanisms, biting behavior, and vector density. *($370,000)*

Indoor Residual Spraying

NMCP/PMI objectives

The NMCP's IRS strategy is influenced in part by its Strategic Plan and in part by its IVM strategy. Specifically, given Rwanda's success in achieving universal LLIN coverage and maintaining high net use, IRS is to be utilized in addition to LLINs in areas where the burden of malaria is greatest (as measured by health facility test positivity rates and entomological indicators such as entomological inoculation rates). PMI supports this evidence-based approach and will continue to review HMIS and entomologic data to determine where best to deploy IRS. To date, only pyrethroids have been used in IRS activities in Rwanda.

Progress during the last 12 months

Table 2 shows PMI/Rwanda's support of IRS implementation since 2007.

Table 2. Coverage with IRS, 2007–2013

Round	Date	Districts	No. of structures sprayed (% targeted structures sprayed)
1	Aug-Sep 2007	Kigali (all three districts)	152,072 (96%)
2	Aug-Sep 2008	Kigali + Nyanza (South Province) and Kirehe (East Province)	189,756 (94%)
3	Jan-Feb 2009	Kigali, Nyanza, and Kirehe	191,051 (97%)
4	Aug-Sep 2009	Kigali, Nyanza, and Kirehe + Bugesera (East Province) and Nyagatare (East Province)	295,174 (98%)
5	Mar 2010	2 Kigali districts (Gasabo and Kicukiro)	63,395(87%)
6	Sep-Oct 2010	Kigali, Nyanza, Kirehe, Bugesera, and Nyagatare	303,659 (99%)
7	Aug-Oct 2011	Nyanza, Kirehe, Bugesera, Nyagatare, and Gisagara	358,804 (98.6%)
8	Aug-Oct 2012	Bugesera, Nyagatare, and Gisagara	236,610 (97.5%)
9	Feb-Mar 2013	Bugesera, Nyagatare, and Gisagara	121,154 (99.6%)

Spraying is reserved for high-burden sectors based on entomologic and epidemiologic data. In 2012, IRS was able to be withdrawn from Kirehe and Nyanza Districts as a result of significant declines in malaria cases. In September 2012, the eighth round of spraying was implemented in three districts: Nyagatare, Bugesera, and Gisagara, and targeted 242,589 structures. Residual IRS efficacy data shows six months of protection. With nine months of transmission, the NMCP and PMI decided to re-spray a portion of the structures (approximately 120,000) in February 2013, to provide protection throughout the entire transmission season. In response to the GPIRM and given the established resistance to pyrethroids, the NMCP decided to move to carbamates as an interim measure until the current ban on organophosphates is lifted. Therefore, carbamates will be used in the September/October 2013 spray round. However, selection of insecticides for future spray rounds will be based on the results of insecticide susceptibility testing and in consultation with the PMI IRS/Entomology team. According to a representative from the Ministry of Agriculture at the NMCP's vector control technical working group, \there is currently a ban on the importation of the organophosphate insecticide. This insecticide has been showing a residual effect of 6-9 months in Ghana and elsewhere. The NMCP is currently verifying this information before submitting a formal request to lift the ban.

PMI was not able to transition components of IRS activities directly to GOR with FY 2012 funds. However, it is anticipated that this will happen with FY 2013 funds. In preparation for this transition, PMI supported a technical/programmatic capacity assessment of GOR in 2013; the final report was shared with the NMCP for final inputs in August 2013. In addition, a fiduciary risk assessment was conducted in early 2012 and a risk mitigation strategy will be incorporated into the bilateral agreement.

Plans and justification

PMI will continue to deploy IRS based on sound local evidence of disease eco-epidemiology, ongoing insecticide susceptibility testing and with continued emphasis on capacity building. Spraying with FY 2014 funds will mark the second year of transitioning components of IRS activities directly to GOR. While the IRS targets for FY 2014 are still subject to changes due to the move from pyrethroids to carbamates (which are six times more expensive), it is envisaged that the Rwandan government will cover approximately 250,000 structures with receipt of $2.5 million from PMI for this purpose. The NMCP estimates their cost per structure sprayed at $10 excluding insecticide. As stated in FY 2013 MOP, with PMI support, the GOR will assume responsibility for implementation of IRS activities, including payment of IRS spray staff, transport, payment of services for spray staff, warehouse and site management, and mobilizer supplies. The PMI implementing partner will retain responsibility for procurement of insecticide, equipment (including protective gear), technical assistance for supervision and environmental monitoring in all three districts. The FY 2014 MOP will also mark the introduction of organophosphates in one district, provided that the current ban in organophosphates is lifted.

Challenges, opportunities, and threats

Recent experience of using carbamates for IRS in other African countries has shown a very low residual effect of the insecticide, varying between 1 to 3 months depending on the type of walls. Use of carbamates will require spraying at least twice a year with an insecticide, six times more expensive than pyrethroids, which would result in a significant decrease in the number of structures that can be sprayed with available funds. This challenge will remain even if the NMCP eventually moves to a longer-lasting insecticide, such as the long-lasting organophosphate.Currently it is almost 13 times more expensive than pyrethroids and more than twice as expensive as carbamates. However, the NMCP and PMI would like to phase to one spray round per year if the duration of the residual efficacy of the organophosphate is adequate. Cost savings will occur with moving to one spray round and the transition of IRS implementation to the GOR.

Proposed activities with FY 2014 funding (7,546,825)

- Support spraying of an annual number of 250,000 structures in high malaria incidence sectors located in three high-burden districts, as determined by HMIS data. The choice of insecticide will be based on results of ongoing insecticide susceptibility testing. Operational costs are based on previous expenditure analyses of the NMCP and assume $10 per structure sprayed. Funds going to the implementing partner will be used to provide technical assistance on environmental compliance and other relevant areas and will also be used to procure insecticides, spraying equipment, and personal protective equipment, whereas funds going to GoR will be used to support spray operations in three districts. Entomologic monitoring (including routine bioassays) is covered under the General Vector Control Section and will continue to guide decision-making on IRS moving forward. *($5,034,725 to partner; $2,500,000 to GoR)*

- Technical assistance for IRS. CDC staff will conduct one TA visit to assist with IRS planning and implementation. *($12,100)*

Insecticide-treated Nets

NMCP/PMI objectives

Having achieved universal coverage of LLINs in February 2011 after a rolling universal campaign, the primary objective is to maintain universal coverage and achieve over 90% use in children under five and pregnant women through:

- continuous distribution channels: ANC, EPI, and schools (to begin in 2013) and;
- universal coverage mass campaigns in 2013 and 2016.

The NMCP defines universal coverage as one net for every two people. Surveys are conducted by CHWs quarterly to quantify LLIN needs by household. Rwanda's national LLIN target elucidated in their 2013 – 2017 MSP is to achieve and maintain over 90% ownership and use.

Challenges, opportunities, and threats

The primary challenge in Rwanda is to maintain universal coverage through continuous distribution to new cohorts of children under five, pregnant women, schoolchildren, and through periodic mass campaigns, which will require adequate financing, forecasting, surveillance, and distribution. The NMCP also has to ensure proper and consistent use of LLINs in the context of reduced malaria burden and possible reduced perceptions of risk.

In 2012, Rwanda distributed approximately 3.2 million LLINs in a targeted rolling campaign which targeted high-burden districts and priority populations like children under five. In 2013, Rwanda will have the opportunity to document best practices and lessons learned about how to maintain universal coverage through mass campaigns and continuous distribution. Interestingly, Rwanda HMIS data has shown malaria increases every two years following an LLIN mass campaign (i.e. there were significant increases in cases in 2009 and again in 2013), which could possibly result from lack of LLIN durability and subsequent loss of impact.

The NMCP is also concerned about problems with LLIN disposal. Thus, PMI will support an assessment of LLIN disposal in Rwanda to determine whether LLIN disposal/recycling are programmatic issues that need to be addressed, or whether people are instead repurposing LLINs safely and effectively during upcoming mass campaigns. The data gathered will provide insight into whether this is a problem that needs to be addressed with the development and implementation of a LLIN disposal strategy. The study will also contribute to the discussions on these issues at the international level.

Major threats facing malaria control and LLINs in Rwanda are established pyrethroid resistance in the Eastern province and lack of durability of LLINs in the field. At the moment, the only insecticide recommended for LLINs is pyrethroids, primarily permethrin, alpha-cypermethrin, and deltamethrin. Resistance testing has confirmed pyrethroid resistance in one high malaria burden district with 18% and 20% mortality to permethrin and deltamethrin respectively. This district has achieved universal LLIN coverage and the NMCP and PMI are implementing IRS with carbamates to mitigate the problem of pyrethroid resistance and conserve the efficacy of the LLIN.

Another challenge is that preliminary results of a longitudinal prospective study of LLIN durability in the field seem to suggest that over 50% of the LLINs fail in terms of holes (proportional hole index >768) within 24 months. Although residual insecticide efficacy is decreasing, bioassays and colorimetric field testing (CFT) show that the efficacy remains above the 80% WHO threshold at 24 months. These observations highlight the need to conduct LLIN efficacy and durability studies to guide strategies to maintain universal coverage of effective LLINs. Results of this study will be disseminated and compared to other net durability studies being conducted throughout PMI countries, and field data will be shared with the WHO LLIN working group for consideration. PMI is working with the NMCP to include net care messaging in their IEC/BCC interventions.

Progress during the last 12 months

In 2012, PMI procured 1,000,500 LLINs to maintain universal coverage through continuous distribution and to respond to an emergency order at the request of the Minister of Health to fill a gap from delays in the procurement of Global Fund nets. PMI is procuring and will distribute a total of 400,000 LLINs and will distribute them in early 2014.

The LLIN impact on Rwanda's malaria burden appears to be significant. Following achievement of universal coverage in 2011, the HMIS showed unprecedented reductions in malaria morbidity and mortality with concomitant increases in LLIN ownership and use. However, during late 2012 and early 2013, over two years since the last LLIN mass distribution campaign, the HMIS is showing increases in the number of malaria cases, as well as an increase in total number of outpatients, this might relate to loss of efficacy due to lack of durability. The NMCP is responding with targeted LLIN distributions in sectors with these malaria case increases. In January 2013, LLINs were targeted to a sector with increasing malaria cases and distributed to children under five in Nygatare by a mass campaign soon after the LLINs arrived in country.

PMI provided external technical assistance to the NMCP to identify, quantify, and forecast viable continuous distribution channels in Rwanda with the NETCALC™ software, which assists in LLIN quantification and forecasting. This continuous distribution workshop also explored different ideas and challenges in maintaining universal coverage through continuous distribution, mass distribution, and private sector sales. In principle, if continuous distribution channels are robust and successful, mass campaigns could be phased out. Yet, Rwanda has achieved and maintained universal coverage with a combination of mass campaigns and continuous distribution through ANC and EPI clinics. School distributions are being piloted in late 2013. The private sector for LLINs is virtually nonexistent in Rwanda. Therefore, the NMCP, PMI, and other stakeholders will continue to implement mass campaigns specifically in 2013/2014 and continuous distribution to target new cohorts through ANC and EPI and pilot school-based distribution given the limited time before 2015, when Rwanda will be evaluated on its progress towards the MDGs and Abuja targets. Following 2015, Rwanda will evaluate different LLIN distribution channels to maximize efficiency and impact.

In 2013, PMI supported technical assistance and data management for a **nationwide** MIS to obtain current LLIN ownership and coverage data. The MIS also included multiple LLIN preference and perception questions. These results will inform LLINs specifications (i.e., conical rather than rectangular and preferred colors) and distribution to increase acceptance and adherence. With decreasing malaria burden, there is evidence that net use is decreasing since many no longer perceive malaria as a risk. As is evidenced in 2009 and 2012, malaria cases can increase and maintaining high LLIN ownership and use is critical for Rwanda's goal of pre-elimination. Therefore, PMI will continue to support the NMCP to work with local civil society organizations to target the CHWs nationwide to carry out interpersonal communication sessions, community mobilization, and sensitization of the population to ensure net use and net care.

Figure 9. Preliminary results of 2011-2012 assessment of the peripheral malaria prevalence in pregnancy, by transmission setting and type of test

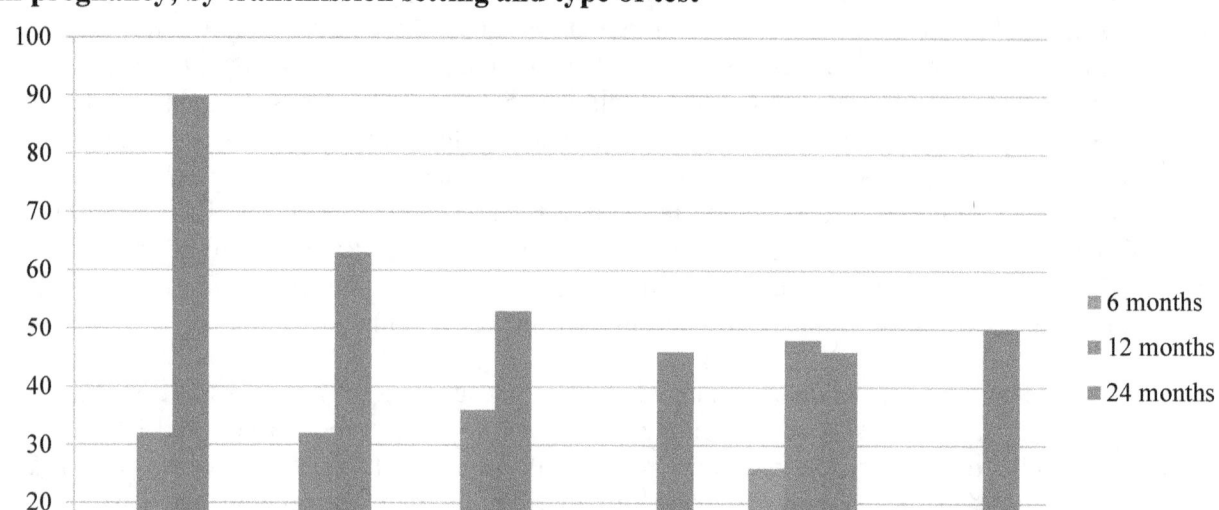

LLIN gap analysis

The NMCP follows the Roll Back Malaria Harmonization Working Group recommendations for LLIN procurement: planning to achieve 100% coverage (or a procurement ratio adjusted for rounding of 1.8 persons per net).

To maintain universal coverage, the NMCP's policy calls for replacement of old, expired LLINs every three years through phased rolling mass campaigns, which use malaria incidence trends to target high-risk districts. The NMCP also prioritizes distribution to high-risk vulnerable and new populations with new delivery channels. In January 2013, LLINs were distributed to children under five in Nygatare soon after arrival in country.

According to the gap analysis below, which takes into account the RBM-recommended attrition rates of 8%, 20% and 50% for years 1, 2, and 3 respectively, Rwanda shows a net gap for 2013 with the universal coverage campaign which PMI will contribute to in FY 2013.

Estimated projection of LLIN needs and gaps, 2013 – 2016

Target groups and delivery channels	CY2013	CY2014	CY2015	CY2016
Population[1]	11,686,013	12,022,635	12,365,180	12,713,052
Infants reached through health facility EPI services (4%)	479,928	492,928	506,972	521,235
Primiparous pregnant women	233,720	240,453	247,304	254,261

	2013	2014	2015	2016
reached through health facility ANC (2%)				
Universal coverage (1 net per 2 people or 1.8 persons per net)	6,492,229			7,062,807
Continuous distribution through schools		1,007,986	643,393	
Total LLIN requirements[2]	7,205,877	1,741,367	1,397,669	7,838,303
Gap of nets from previous year		1,956,257	85,720	0
Effective nets[3]	2,547,145	2,182,560	1,534,672	714,672
Total estimated LLINs needed	**4,658,732**	**1,515,064**	**(51,283)**	**7,123,631**
	Planned LLIN Contributions			
Source	**2013**	**2014**	**2015**	**2016**
Estimated PMI support	400,000	1,000,000	375,000	
Global Fund Round 8	429,344 1,873,131	429,344		
Total available	2,702,475	1,429,344	**375,000**	
Total estimated gap	**1,956,257**	**85,720**	**379,276 (routine coverage)**	**7,123,631**

*Of those nets, 500,000 were procured in response to an emergency

[1]National Institute of Statistics of Rwanda, National Population Projection 2007-2022, July 2009.
[2]Replacement of net needs are calculated at 1 net for every 2 people or a ratio of 1.8 persons per net (per RBM HWG recommendations).).
[3] Loss rates of nets are calculated based on RBM HWG recommendations (8% year 1, 20% year 2 and 50% year 3)

Plans and justification

PMI will support the maintenance of universal coverage with the procurement and distribution of LLINs, support net durability assessment of LLIN innovations, and support for BCC campaigns to dispel misperceptions of malaria risk and promote usage. PMI will procure 1,000,000 LLINs with FY 2013 funds (described above) to contribute to maintaining universal coverage and to address LLIN gaps/needs in CY2013, including reaching targeted vulnerable populations through specific delivery channels. Global Fund single source funding will cover procurement of 429,344 LLINs in 2014. Although the current gap analysis does not show a LLIN gap in 2015, this is mainly due to the effective nets remaining from the Universal Coverage campaign. In order to maintain routine coverage of new nets every year, PMI/Rwanda plans to procure up to 375,000 LLINs with FY 2014 funds to contribute to the ANC/EPI and prepare to respond to the large gap in CY 2016. This will also provide a buffer given the uncertainties of timing for funding regarding the Global Fund after June 2014 in Rwanda. If current Global Fund commitments are met and these LLINs are not needed, any excess in funding will be reprogrammed or combined with FY 2015 funds to mitigate the anticipated huge gap in 2016.

Given the usefulness of the results from the net durability study and the capacity built within the NMCP, PMI would also like to continue net durability testing to test innovations in LLINs such as new materials or new insecticide combinations in field settings.

Proposed activities with FY 2014 funding ($2,646,000)

PMI will support NMCP's efforts to maintain universal LLIN coverage by procuring and distributing LLINs for distribution through continuous distribution, phased rolling mass campaigns, and new delivery channels targeting vulnerable populations. PMI will also support an assessment to determine if LLIN disposal is a problem or are LLINs being repurposed appropriately. If issues are noted, PMI will provide technical assistance to develop and implement a disposal strategy. PMI will also support focused BCC efforts at national and community levels to promote correct and consistent usage (described under BCC) especially given the reducing burden and reduced risk perception. Specific activities for Year 8 include:

- *Procure and distribute 375,000 LLINs*: Support the procurement and distribution of free LLINs through continuous distribution channels for distribution targeting first-time pregnant women and newborns based on the gap analysis. Other potential channels to vulnerable groups include orphanages, boarding schools, and in-patients at hospitals depending on the NMCP's strategy. PMI has identified biodegradable packaging options with partners and net manufactures that will not require repackaging of the bags at health centers or during mass campaigns. *($2,214,750))*

- *MPDD management fee for 375,000 LLINs*: MPDD charges an 8% management fee for malaria commodities procured with USG funds; the fee covers import and storage. *($177,200))*

- *Distribution of 375,000 LLINs*: The MPDD has distributed Global Fund–procured LLINs for mass campaigns with significant support from the National Police. Therefore, an additional $0.50 per LLIN is included to provide transportation to the health center and subsequently to the community. *($188,000))*

- *Technical assistance for LLINs*: With the implementation of the campaign to maintain universal coverage and replace failed ITNs, Rwanda has questions such as how to best maintain universal coverage and how to dispose/recycle nets distributed through universal campaigns once they fail. Technical assistance will be provided to respond to emerging issues in universal LLIN coverage and disposal. *($25,000)*

- *Net durability and insecticide resistance monitoring.* Prospective LLIN durability, longevity, and efficacy monitoring of new net products (polypropylene combination nets). *($60,000)*

- *Community mobilization and health communications for LLIN use:* PMI will support NMCP's efforts to work with CHWs and established local NGOs to carry out interpersonal communication sessions, community mobilization, and sensitization across all malaria interventions. (included in BCC section)

Malaria in Pregnancy

NMCP/PMI objectives

NMCP MIP interventions include providing an LLIN to every primigravidae on her first visit to an antenatal care (ANC) clinic, low-dose iron/folate tablets for all pregnant women, and effective case management of pregnant women with fever, after parasitological diagnosis by microscopy or RDTs.

With PMI support, the MOH Maternal Child Health (MCH) desk has coordinated with the NMCP, the CHD, and EPI to integrate and strengthen program implementation. The services provided by these units, in addition to fetal growth monitoring and birth preparation, comprise the focused antenatal care (FANC) package, which is implemented nationwide.

Challenges, opportunities, and threats

Rwanda stopped supporting IPTp in 2008, but is now considering a switch to a new approach to preventing and controlling malaria in pregnancy: intermittent screen and treat (IST). NMCP will review the results of IST studies in other countries to determine if it is the right approach for Rwanda.

Progress during the last 12 months

The MoH, with the support of partners including PMI, has worked to improve the quality of FANC services at health facilities through training and capacity-building efforts at national and district levels. In 2012, PMI continued FANC and ASM support in 13 of the 30 districts; other districts were supported by Global Fund. FANC supervision and refresher training of those trained last year was conducted, and 74% of the FANC trained providers were validated as competent in offering FANC services. New FANC trainings in five districts trained 265 providers out of the 270 targeted.

PMI has also supported trainings to strengthen the role of ASMs in malaria in pregnancy in 2012. Eighty-two supervisors in two districts were trained as trainers and then through a cascade training program, 913 ASMs in those two districts were also trained. The trainings were integrated with the MCH program. After the trainings, ASMs reported an increase in confidence in providing education to pregnant women in terms of sleeping under an LLIN, birth preparedness, danger signs during pregnancy including malaria (i.e. fever while pregnant), the importance of going to a health center for delivery, and the importance of prenatal visits. During the same period, 178 previously trained ASMs from a different district were supervised using a new integrated CHW supervision tool, which includes supervision on malaria activities. Training materials developed in the previous year were implemented and put to use in the health facilities located in the 13 districts that received PMI support in 2012. The materials were designed to help strengthen integrated ANC services including FANC, prevention of mother-to-child transmission of HIV, nutrition education, promotion of breast-feeding, and family planning.

Rapid assessment of the burden of malaria in pregnancy

The study of the burden of malaria in pregnancy was completed in 2012 and a final report is expected in the fall of 2013 (Figure 9). The study was conducted in six sites with varying malaria endemicity and targeted both primigravidae and multigravidae at their first ANC visit. Peripheral malaria parasitemia was measured with microscopy, RDTs, and PCR. Pregnant women were also asked about LLIN ownership and use. Preliminary survey results show that malaria prevalence in pregnant women by microscopy was approximately 2%, 3% and 6% at the national level for microscopy, RDT, and PCR respectively (Figure 9). High transmission settings (Nygatare and Gisagara) had the highest prevalence: 5%, 7%, 13% by microscopy, RDT, and PCR respectively. The figure below illustrates the district variability of prevalence by type of test and transmission setting.

Figure 9. Preliminary results of 2011-12 assessment of the peripheral malaria burden in pregnancy, by transmission setting and type of test

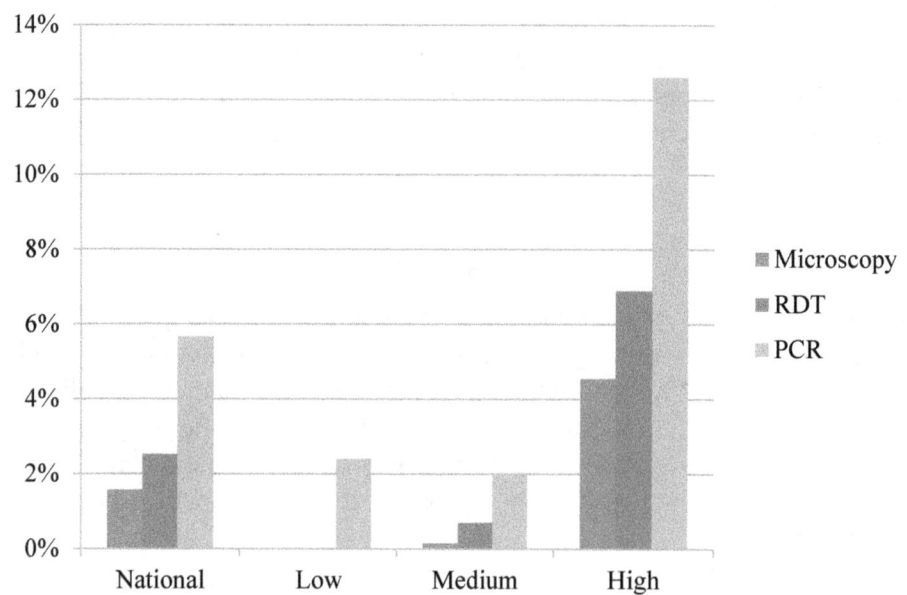

Plans and justification

The NMCP is re-evaluating their MIP approach for inclusion in the 2013-2017 Malaria Strategic Plan. Results of the rapid assessment showed a relatively low nationwide malaria prevalence of approximately 2% in pregnant women by microscopy, which supports the significant decline in malaria cases observed over the last years. However, the study highlighted a higher burden of malaria (4.8% by microscopy) in pregnant women in malaria districts with higher levels of transmission, which exacerbates birth and maternal outcomes. In order to reduce this burden, the NMCP is considering the implementation of IST with RDTs during ANC visits. The NMCP is waiting for results of IST studies being conducted in other countries to determine the efficacy and feasibility of implementing this approach. Their vision is to implement IST in three high malaria burden districts and monitor and evaluate impact of this approach in reducing the burden of MIP in Rwanda. For FY 2014, the NMCP will continue to distribute LLINs to all primigravid women in their first ANC visit, implement FANC to ensure quality care, and engage and mobilize ASMs to encourage early and frequent ANC attendance to promote a healthy delivery.

Proposed activities with FY 2014 funding ($200,000)

- *Implementation of malaria in pregnancy interventions at community, district, and national levels*: PMI will continue to support MCH and malaria interventions for pregnant women by providing technical assistance for MIP strategy development, coordination for strategy implementation at the national level, and resources for trainings as needed at the district level. PMI, in coordination with USG MCH programs and the MOH, will also continue to support FANC services, including the supervision of ASMs by health center supervisors; the training of ASMs; printing of training materials and routine data collection tools; evaluation of community outreach to pregnant women; and strengthening the linkage between ASMs and health facilities to promote early detection and treatment of malaria in pregnancy, LLIN use, and ANC attendance by pregnant women. *($200,000)*

Case Management

Diagnosis

NMCP/PMI objectives

Rwanda's national malaria treatment policy states that all suspect cases of malaria should be laboratory confirmed by either microscopy or RDT prior to treatment with an ACT. The policy applies to all age groups and health facilities, communities, and the private sector. The diagnostic policy advocates the use of microscopy in health facilities and limits the role of RDTs in health facilities to use in emergency situations and at times when laboratory technicians are not available. RDTs have been introduced nationwide for use by CHWs for parasitological confirmation of malaria cases.

Progress since the launch of PMI

Diagnostic capacity is a critical component of malaria case management particularly in the context of Rwanda's rapidly decreasing malaria transmission and changing epidemiology. Rwanda has made remarkable progress to ensure appropriate malaria diagnosis before treatment with ACTs. With PMI and Global Fund support, Rwanda achieved greater than 90% laboratory confirmation of malaria cases (HMIS, 2011). With PMI support, the National Reference Laboratory (NRL) conducts supervision of district hospital staff and maintains internal QA/QC for microscopy.

Progress during the last 12 months

In 2012, the NRL completed standard operating procedures (SOPs) for malaria diagnosis, external quality control, and slide preparation; conducted a 10-day advanced training for 11 lab technologists from referral and district hospitals and seven 5-day basic malaria microscopy training sessions for lab technicians from health centers and district hospitals in Nyagatare (n=15) and Kirehe (n=16) and 72 parasitology staff from Rutongo, Kibilizi, Rwamagana, and Muhima District Hospitals and the Rwanda Military Hospital; conducted proficiency testing and corrective supervision in all 42 district hospitals; and supported two NRL staff members to participate in a refresher training on malaria microscopy in Kisumu, Kenya.

The change to universal diagnostic testing has resulted in increased attention to provider behavior, and 502 health providers have been trained or provided refresher courses on IMCI. Monthly supervisory visits from district health staff to health centers have been conducted.

In 2012, PMI procured 500,000 RDTs, 150,000 safety boxes for needle disposal, as well as 85 microscopes and supplies for use in health facilities. In addition, PMI has supported the training of 1,435 CHWs in malaria diagnosis and treatment and 354 ASMs in diagnostics (RDTs) thus far in 2013. Results of assessments show that CHWs adhere to negative test results and do not treat the patient for malaria.

RDT gap analysis, 2013 – 2015

	2013	2014	2015
Percentage of fever cases diagnosed as clinical malaria in outpatient	2,760,000 (92%)	2,842,800 (92%)	2,928,084 (92%)
Country target for diagnostic coverage	100%	100%	100%
% diagnostic coverage by microscopy	80%	80%	80%
% diagnostic coverage by RDT	20%	20%	20%
% coverage of public sector by RDTs	30%	30%	20%
% coverage of community by RDTs	70%	70%	70%
% coverage of private sector by RDTs (through insurance companies)	0%	0%	10%
Need in RDT	594,000	611,820	630,175
RDT needed for IST during MIP		452,359	465,025

RDT needed for epidemic situations		61,182	63,018
Total RDTs needed		**1,125,361**	**1,158,218**
Buffer stock	96,000	131,292	131,292
Total RDTs needed	**690,000**	**1,256,653**	**1,289,510**
Available RDTs (already financed from any source)		825,040	
Available RDTs (already financed from any source) from PMI	500,000	1,162,000	
Excess in RDTs from previous year			730,387
Final gap of RDTs needed	**190,000**	**-730,387**	**559,123**

Challenges, opportunities, and threats

The agreement between PMI/Rwanda and the NRL ended on May 31, 2013, and future laboratory QA/QC activities will be conducted at district level under the coordination of the NMCP through government-to-government funding. The NMCP is well placed to support decentralized QA/QC activities at the district level.

Plans and justification

Although the above gap analysis only shows a gap of 559,123 RDTs in 2015, as requested by the NMCP, PMI/Rwanda plans to procure up to 1.2 million RDTs given the increasing trends in malaria cases in 2012/2013, the possibility of expanding iCCM to older age groups, and uncertainties regarding the Global Fund after June 2014 in Rwanda. If Global Fund commitments are met and RDTs are not needed, funding will be reprogrammed or combined with FY 2015 funds to mitigate the anticipated large gap in 2016. PMI support for the quality control of microscopy and RDTs will be provided directly to the district hospitals by the NMCP and the National Reference Laboratory and to the health centers by the district hospitals.

Proposed activities with FY 2014 funding ($1,338,000)

- *Strengthen malaria laboratory diagnostics in health facilities*: PMI will continue to strengthen malaria diagnostics by supporting an integrated and decentralized national quality control system for microscopy at health facilities and providing continued training for malaria diagnostics including RDTs. PMI will reinforce training at health facility level. Training needs will be ascertained through the quality control system. *($100,000)*

- *Procure microscopes and laboratory consumables*: PMI has been supporting the MoH policy for mandatory laboratory confirmation before ACT treatment. PMI will continue this support by procuring microscopes and laboratory consumables. *($50,000)*

- *Procure approximately 1,200,000 RDTs and 50,000 safety boxes*: PMI has been supporting procurement of RDTs for use by CHWs in communities. With the ending of the current Global Fund grants in June 2014, PMI will increase its contribution for RDTs and safety boxes. PMI will also support customs clearance, storage, and transport. *($1,188,000)*

Treatment

NMCP/PMI objectives

As of October 2006, all health facilities officially transitioned the first-line treatment for uncomplicated malaria from amodiaquine-SP to artemether-lumefantrine (AL). Oral quinine is recommended when AL is contraindicated, such as in children weighing less than 5 kilograms and pregnant women in their first trimester, and as the second-line treatment for cases of uncomplicated malaria when AL is not well tolerated or available. In 2011, Rwanda changed its treatment policy for the first-line treatment of severe malaria from parenteral quinine to parenteral artesunate; parenteral quinine and parenteral artemether remain as second-line alternatives. Intramuscular artesunate is recommended as pre-referral treatment for the management of severe malaria in health facilities only.

In 2004, the MOH CHD introduced and consolidated the iCCM package to include malaria, pneumonia, diarrhea, and other components (e.g., nutrition, family planning, hygiene, palliative care) in six districts. Currently, approximately 30,000 CHWs implement the iCCM package throughout the country's 30 districts. PMI Rwanda supports iCCM in seven districts and also assists the NMCP by repackaging ACTs for the community sector with pictorial dosing information. There is no policy to date for pre-referral treatment for the management of severe malaria at the community level although discussions are ongoing and the NMCP is considering a study to determine the feasibility of rectal artesunate (Malaria Program Review, p. 46).

Progress since the launch of PMI

Because the Global Fund has been providing ACTs for use in health facilities, PMI has supported refresher trainings and supervisory visits from the NMCP and district staff have been trained to promote the implementation of quality Integrated Management of Childhood Illness (IMCI) in health facilities.

Rwanda has a well-established community-based health system for the management of malaria, diarrhea, and pneumonia. Financing of the community-based health care is provided through the community insurance scheme, small fees collected for medications, and community performance-based financing. Rwanda has successfully scaled up the use of RDTs by CHWs.

Progress during the last 12 months

Antimalarials for health facilities continue to be covered mostly under Global Fund. However, NMCP asked PMI for an emergency procurement of 300,000 ACT treatments because the delivery of Global-Fund procured ACTs was delayed. With the policy change to universal diagnostic testing, increased attention has been focused on provider behavior. In 2012, PMI supported refresher training and supervision of health care providers in eight districts.

In 2012, PMI continued support to IMCI through training of 3,098 community health workers (CHWs) in malaria treatment with ACTs. Additional support included supervision of 356 CHW binomes and provision of revised iCCM tools to 2,692 CHWs and basic iCCM kits to 1,948 CHWs. Finally, in 2012, PMI supported the first consignment of 40,000 vials of parenteral artesunate and will procure additional 62,000 vials with FY 2013 funds for the treatment of severe malaria.

Gap analysis for ACTs 2012 – 2015

ACTs Needs by Sector	2012	2013	2014	2015	2016
ACT consumption data	428,001	477,934	465,451	457,961	457,961
Target coverage by sector					
Health facility	66%	58%	56%	51%	51%
Community	34%	34%	34%	34%	34%
Private	0%	8%	10%	15%	15%
Number of malaria cases by sector					
Health Facility	282,481	277,202	260,653	233,560	233,560
Community Case Management	145,520	162,498	158,253	155,707	155,707
Private	0	38,235	46,545	68,694	68,694
Sub total	**428,001**	**477,934**	**465,451**	**457,961**	**457,961**
ACTs for efficacy study		500		500	
ACTs for epidemics		16,513	14,082	14,720	13,800

ACTs for IST		16,605	17,037	17,480	17,934
Total	**428,001**	**511,552**	**496,570**	**490,661**	**489,965**
Annual buffer stock (20%)	85,600	102,310	99,314	98,132	97,993
Total	**513,601**	**613,862**	**595,884**	**588,793**	**587,958**
Commitments					
GF	787,373*	574,720	270,344		
PMI		300,000**	30,000		
Excess ACTs from previous year		273,772	534,630	**239,090**	
Updated gap	-273,772	-534,630	-239,090	349,703	587,958

*Delayed
**Emergency request by the NMCP

Challenges, opportunities, and threats

Despite Rwanda's remarkable progress in ensuring appropriate malaria diagnosis before treatment with ACTs, there were ACT stock outs in the last quarter of 2012 caused by delay in arrival of GF ACTs, especially those targeted for use at the community level. PMI was able to respond to a ministerial emergency ACT request by procuring 300,000 ACTs not planned in 2013. The stockouts also created an opportunity for MPDD, NMCP, and PMI to further improve data sharing and transparent forecasting and planning.

There is no pre-referral treatment policy for severe malaria in the community, because the use of rectal suppositories would not be well accepted by communities. With PMI support, an assessment of the acceptability of rectal suppositories for the pre-referral management of severe malaria in the community in children under five years old is proposed and will be planned as an operational research question that needs to be answered.

Plans and justification

PMI will continue to support prompt and effective case management of malaria through provision of ACTs for use by CHWs and parenteral artesunate for the treatment of severe malaria in health facilities. This contribution will help fill the gap left by the Global Fund in these commodities in 2014/2015.

Proposed activities with FY 2014 funding ($2,952,275)

- *Procure malaria drugs*: PMI will procure 350,000 ACT treatments and 45,000 vials of parenteral artesunate for severe malaria, to address the gap left by Global Fund in 2013/2014. *($336,412)*

- *Management and distribution of malaria treatments*: Costing estimates approximately 8% to deliver supplies. *($26,913)*

- *Supervision of health facility workers by NMCP*: Provide support to NMCP for supervision at district hospitals and health facilities. *($150,000)*

- *Support for integrated community case management implementation*: PMI will continue to support implementation of the iCCM package in seven districts. The support will include original and refresher trainings at district levels, supportive supervision, training in appropriate RDT use, evaluating CHW performance with RDTs, monitoring activities, and provision of CHW materials and supplies. PMI will support CHWs to provide appropriate health communications messages to encourage understanding and adherence to the current treatment algorithms. PMI, with leveraged funds from other USG MCH programs, will support the complete package of iCCM interventions, which includes malaria, pneumonia, diarrhea, malnutrition, and family planning, in currently supported districts or other districts depending on priorities of the MOH. *($2,000,000)*

- *Technical assistance for iCCM implementation*: Although PMI will support iCCM implementation in seven districts, general technical assistance for iCCM implementation will be provided nationwide including strengthening supervision, quality control of diagnostics, and M&E. *($100,000)*

- *Support for third-year Peace Corps Volunteer (PCV)*: As part of the ongoing collaboration with Peace Corps, PMI will continue support up to two third-year PCVs for placement with the iCCM implementing partner. The PCVs will live in Kigali and work out of the implementing partner's office with regular (at least once a week) site visits to multiple communities within one district. Their responsibilities will include mentoring and supporting CHWs and their supervisors in each of three to five communities in one district. This will allow cross-fertilization across communities of ideas, best practices, and lessons learned. Other duties may include piloting new interventions or systems; compiling and disseminating lessons learned and best practices to the central level; and working closely with health center supervisors in ongoing trainings, routine supervision visits, quality assurance of diagnostics, case management, reporting, stock management, behavior change communication and monthly meetings. Technical supervision will be provided by a PMI Resident Advisor and the implementing partner's technical advisor for iCCM. In addition, the PCVs will be responsible for providing technical support to health PCVs in Rwanda. Costs include housing, a computer, workspace in the central office, local travel and a phone. *($20,000)*

- *Central Level Supply Chain Management*: Strengthen pharmaceutical management and supply chain at the national and district levels with the support of a seconded logistician and technical assistance for coordinated procurement and distribution of malaria

47

commodities (Coordinated Procurement and Distribution System CPDS)), as well as support implementation of the electronic logistics management system (e-LM). *($300,000)*

Monitoring and Evaluation

NMCP/PMI objectives

Rwanda is a data-rich environment and the NMCP, districts, and health centers are using evidence to refine and target malaria control interventions. Rwanda continues on the path toward malaria pre-elimination, defined by WHO as <5% SPR among febrile patients nationwide, with reductions in malaria morbidity and mortality following universal LLIN coverage, IRS in three high-burden districts, and iCCM with RDTs and ACTs. Based on these decreasing trends Rwanda's National Malaria Strategic Plan lays out its focus on achieving pre-elimination by 2017.

In the context of pre-elimination, experts at the malaria forum recommended that Rwanda enhance surveillance and response as it has successfully scaled up interventions and is transitioning from malaria control to pre-elimination. Malaria trends attest to a shifting malaria epidemiology and the NMCP and partners need to adapt to these changes to better target effective interventions, monitor progress, and evaluate impact The transition to pre-elimination will require more vigilance and resources. . PMI will assist Rwanda in evaluating their progress towards the Millennium Development Goals (MDGs) and the Abuja targets in preparation for the 2015 deadline.

Table 3. Rwanda Monitoring and Evaluation Table, 2007 – 2015

Data source	Year								
	2007	2008	2009	2010	2011	2012	2013	2014	2015
Household surveys[1]	Interim DHS with MIS with verbal autopsy			DHS			MIS	DHS	
Other surveys[2]	SPA		TRAC	HFS		TRAC HFS		HFS	
Malaria surveillance and routine system support[3]	Ento HMIS	Ento HMIS DQA	Ento HMIS DQA	Ento HMIS DQA	Ento HMIS DQA	Ento HMIS DQA	Ento HMIS DQA	Ento HMIS DQA	Ento HMIS DQA
Other data sources[4]				Net durabil ity TES	Net durabil ity TES	Net durabilit y TES	Net durabilit y TES	TES	TES

DHS, Demographic and Health Survey; MIS, Malaria Indicator Survey, SPA, Service Provider Assessment; TRAC, Malaria Control Behavioral Tracking Survey; HFS, Health Facility Survey; Ento, Entomologic monitoring and insecticide resistance monitoring; HMIS, Health Management Information System; DQA, Data Quality Assessment; TES, Therapeutic Efficacy Surveillance.

Progress in M&E since PMI Launch

Rwanda has achieved remarkable reductions in the burden of malaria since the inception of PMI (Figure 10). From 2006 to 2011, Rwanda saw an 86% decrease in malaria incidence, an 87% decrease in malaria morbidity, and a 74% decrease in malaria mortality as reported by HMIS (Figure 10). Despite these unprecedented reductions and robust reporting, Rwanda experiences fluctuations in malaria cases. In the first quarter of 2013 (January to March), Rwanda reported over 200,000 confirmed cases, which represent about 92% of the cumulative total for all of 2011 (Figure 11). However, these increases are detectable due to increased diagnostic confirmation of microscopy at health centers, RDTs in the community, a consistently improving HMIS,and are small compared to epidemic threshold modeling based on historical data (Figure 12).

Figure 10. Malaria trends in Rwanda, 2005 – 2011

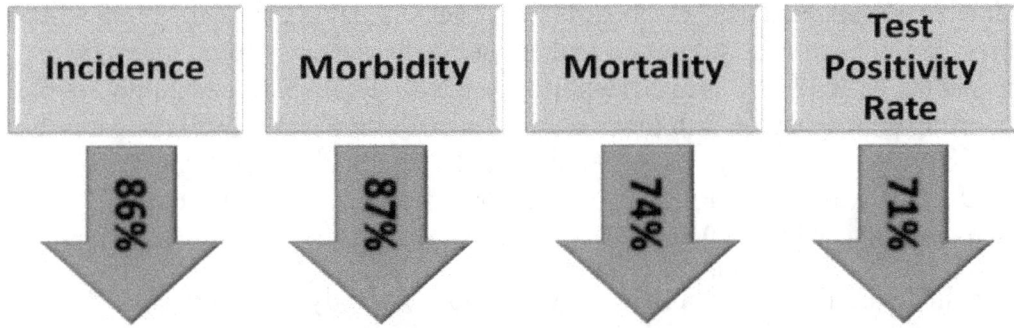

As described above, the fragile nature of malaria control is evidenced by increases in malaria cases occurring in late 2009/early 2010 and in late 2012/early 2013 (Figure 12). These experiences highlight the importance of updating the epidemic thresholds and developing an epidemic detection and response strategy with rationale evidence-based approaches. However, one caveat in preparing for an epidemic is to acknowledge the challenge of setting up epidemic thresholds (usually based on 3-5 year trends) in the context of ongoing reductions in the malaria burden over time. As malaria prevalence abates, epidemic thresholds will need to be continuously revised downward and will require ever higher reporting frequency.

Figure 11. Rwanda Out-Patient Department Malaria Cases (presumed and confirmed), 2006–2012

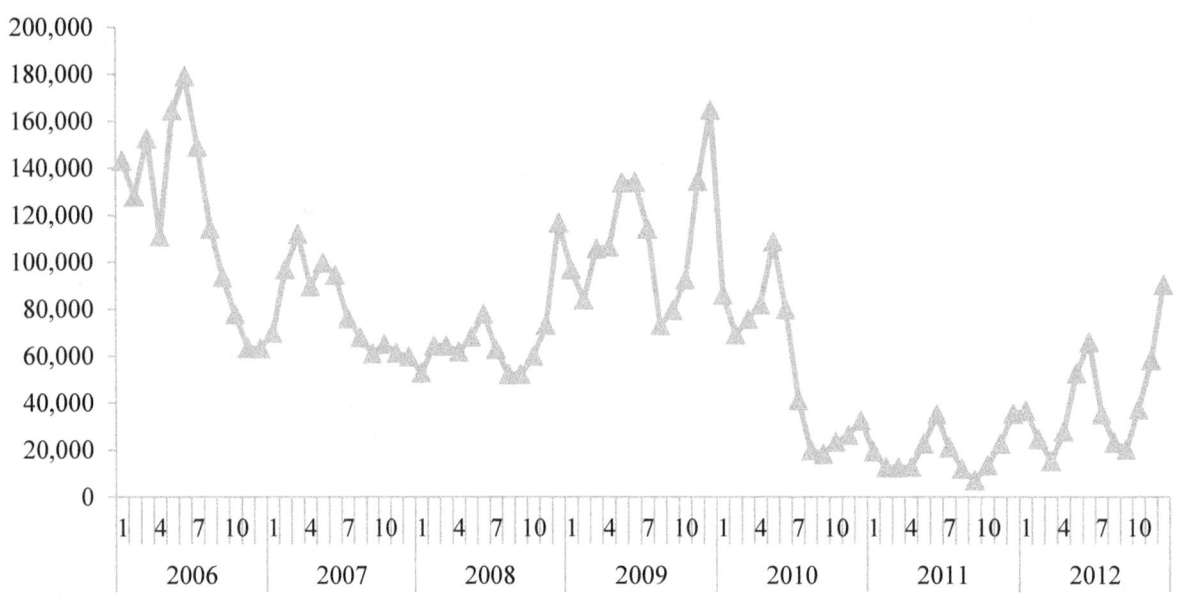

Health facilities report routine data on confirmed malaria cases through the HMIS and CHWs report through SIS-COM (*mUbmizima*). Both systems, which have been supported through PMI and PEPFAR, are vital for tracking malaria trends and were integrated in 2012 under the DHIS2 web-based platform. DHIS2 allows password-restricted web access to PMI resident advisors, NMCP, and other stakeholders and real-time reporting, analysis, and mapping. The NMCP, PMI, and HMIS section have developed data dashboards with relevant malaria indicators to facilitate data analysis, presentation, and timely decision making at the district and central levels by malaria officers and the NMCP. PMI is also supporting the NMCP and partners to pilot mobile phone-based reporting in one district with low malaria burden (TPR<1%) as well the development and implementation of a database to track individual malaria cases in the context of pre-elimination. Districts with low TPRs will be transitioned over time with the aim of community-based surveillance by CHWs.

Data reports are complete, submitted in a timely fashion, and generally of high quality. Reporting is enhanced through performance-based financing (PBF) and over 90% of health centers and CHWs report complete and timely data. Integrated data quality audits are conducted semi-annually through the MoH, and reporting systems include automated logic and cross-checks to ensure data quality.

In 2010, malaria trends were influenced by numerous changes, including implementation of new reporting systems, increased health care utilization with the adoption of health insurance schemes (*mutuelles*), case definition changes, and the rapidly increasing proportion of cases treated in the community with the scale-up of iCCM. However, these decreasing malaria trends have been corroborated over time through HMIS, SIS-COM, and MIS and DHS results.

PMI/Country Progress during last 12 months

Rwanda continues to make progress in monitoring and evaluation, as seen by evidence-based decision-making with data from the HMIS and SIS-COM, a completed 2013 MIS, piloting of mobile reporting and investigation in a low prevalence district, and entomological monitoring. PMI continued to strengthen the NMCP M&E capacity by training HMIS unit staff. DHIS2 has been functional for a year with web-based access and data are being analyzed and reported in a more timely fashion, with increased quality, and increased access through the web-based platform. The NMCP continues to monitor data quality, with PMI support, by conducting semiannual data quality assessments of reported malaria cases. PMI collaborated with the MoH in participating in the annual Global Fund on-site data verification process. Both assessments have found high concurrence between HMIS records and health facility registers.

With the goal of pre-elimination by 2017, the NMCP has prioritized epidemic surveillance and response. This includes enhanced passive surveillance from health facilities, real-time cell phone reporting by CHWs, and subsequent case investigation and follow-up. With the significant reductions in malaria, PMI has also supported the NMCP in mapping and stratifying malaria cases, calculating new epidemic thresholds, and standardizing protocols for epidemic surveillance and response. PMI has also supported the development and finalization of the 2013-2017 Malaria Strategic Plan. The NMCP and partners with PMI support are also in the process of documenting best practices in malaria control with a health system strengthening, impact evaluation, and a Roll Back Malaria (RBM) Progress & Impact series report.

Challenges, opportunities, and threats

Rwanda's new Malaria Strategic Plan 2013 – 2017 reorients the program and updates the M&E plan to specifically focus on building M&E capacity at the district level and enhanced surveillance at the community. Districts will need to coordinate community efforts to identify and respond rationally to upsurges in malaria to achieve and maintain pre-elimination status. Support of this decentralization will also be challenging given that PMI usually supports at a national and central level.

Currently, 19 out of 30 (63%) districts in Rwanda show consistent monthly slide positivity rates (SPRs) of less than five percent among febrile patients even during the peak malaria season. Rwanda will need to expand efforts in these low-burden districts (SPR<5%) and shrink the malaria map. This is possible through the decentralization process prioritized by the MoH and offers the NMCP an opportunity to build district-level capacity and improve malaria control. Major threats, such as insecticide resistance and net failure, are being monitored and an insecticide resistance mitigation strategy has been developed and implemented.

Plans and justification

PMI will continue to support the NMCP to strengthen evidenced-based decision making throughout the health system with the focus on decentralization. PMI will continue to strengthen M&E staff capacity to maintain high quality data, perform data analysis, and make data-based programmatic decisions. On the path towards pre-elimination, Rwanda will need to shift toward enhanced surveillance and epidemic detection and response and move from limited aggregate data to individual reporting and line listings with additional data such as travel history. With decreasing malaria burden and transition from stable endemicity to unstable epidemicity, GoR has prioritized decentralization of data collection and use to increase the ability for districts to analyze and respond to upsurges in malaria. PMI will support the NMCP to sustain decentralized M&E capacity, build a database, and improve the HMIS to ensure that pre-elimination data needs are met. With FY 2014 funds, PMI will also technically support the planning and implementation of a Demographic Health Survey (DHS) in 2014/2015 and a health facility survey to assess intervention coverage and clinical capacity and quality, respectively.

Proposed Activities with FY 2014 Funding ($1,229,200)

- *Expand enhanced community surveillance, case investigation, and epidemic response in five to ten low prevalence districts (those with TPR below 1%) in the context of pre-elimination:* PMI will expand training of CHWs on real-time mobile reporting of confirmed malaria cases in five to ten low prevalence districts. Standardized protocols will be developed, implemented, and disseminated. Support will also be provided to the HMIS to ensure that the system is robust and capable of Rwanda's transition towards pre-elimination. *($600,000)*

- *Provide technical assistance for epidemic response:* PMI will provide technical assistance to the NMCP to develop an updated epidemic surveillance and response strategy with new epidemic thresholds and standard operating procedures for responding. *($25,000)*

- *Support the development and implementation of an enhanced surveillance system:* CDC TDY support will provide technical assistance to the NMCP in developing and implementing an enhanced surveillance system with individual case reporting (rather than aggregate case reporting). *($24,200)*

- *Conduct a progress toward pre-elimination readiness assessment:* PMI will support a team to conduct a readiness assessment to gauge Rwandan's progress toward pre-elimination and provide recommendations on what needs to be improved in order to achieve the goal in 2017. *($50,000)*

- *Implement a 2014/2015 Demographic Health Survey (DHS):* PMI will contribute to the 2014/2015 DHS by providing support to the MoH and technical assistance to monitor Rwanda's progress toward their millennium development goals (MDGs). *($100,000)*

- *Implement a health facility survey in 2014:* PMI will support the NMCP and provide technical assistance to conduct a health facility survey to improve health care worker performance. *($300,000)*

- *Support decentralized M&E capacity at the districts:* PMI will provide technical assistance to train district personnel to analyze malaria data and respond effectively. *($100,000)*

- *M&E reporting systems in USAID/Rwanda*: PMI will contribute to a mission contract for harmonizing partner reporting systems and ensure USAID reporting requirements. The contractor will train implementing partners and collate quarterly data for mission and PMI annual reports. *($100,000)*

Behavior Change Communication (BCC)

NMCP/PMI objectives

Rwanda's National Behavior Change Communication Policy for the Health Sector aims to strengthen the implementation of overall development objectives in Rwanda. This national policy emphasizes enabling the population to make informed health behavior choices through providing appropriate information, using quality messages and methods, including use of media. The 2013–2017 National Malaria Strategic Plan and Rwanda's Malaria Communication Strategy 2010–2012stress the importance of interpersonal communication within the community as the cornerstone of any malaria intervention in Rwanda. Interpersonal communication should build on an "enabling environment" and strengthened health services. All health behavior change activities are under the auspices of the Rwanda Center for Health Communication within the Ministry of Health. This center coordinates, integrates, and harmonizes health messaging across the MoH, working specifically with the NMCP and other programs.

Progress during the last 12 months

In the last year, PMI/Rwanda has supported BCC activities in promoting LLIN use, improving malaria case management, and supporting IRS. In FY 2012, a new bilateral project to plan and conduct BCC activities was awarded and in early 2013 they began to implement activities. . A malaria behavioral tracking survey was conducted in 2012, and the results will be used to revise strategies for FY 2013 and FY 2014.

To promote LLIN use and improve case management nationwide, PMI supported new billboards stressing diagnostics and treatment, mobile video sessions to promote sleeping under a bed net, drama shows on malaria in towns and villages, sessions on how to use malaria treatment drugs, community events on malaria prevention, and interpersonal communication sessions. These efforts resulted in reaching 7,408 people with malaria prevention messages, 136 community events on malaria prevention, 313 interpersonal communication sessions, 397 door-to-door sessions, three sessions of the malaria mobile van cinema, and 106 theater presentations. Additional activities have included the production of tools including flipcharts for use by CHWs, and a campaign with local leaders using community radio.

The following BCC activities were conducted in three districts to increase acceptance and uptake of IRS: community meetings, door-to-door mobilization, use of CHWs and other volunteers to disseminate information about the project, and mass media. Of the houses targeted, 97.5% of the houses accepted spraying in August 2012 and 99.6% in February 2013.

Challenges, opportunities, and threats

Rwanda's success in increasing the scale-up of interventions and in decreasing its malaria burden poses challenges to communications efforts as well as opportunities. When people are aware that malaria transmission has fallen to low levels in most districts, some become complacent, even if they live in districts with higher prevalence. BCC may require a new strategy during this era of malaria pre-elimination as it may become more difficult to capture their attention through mass media and interpersonal communication efforts and to convey their continued malaria risk. Another challenge is that the Rwanda Center for Health Communication has a large portfolio, yet is understaffed. All messages and communications activities must be approved by the center, so occasionally approvals are delayed. BCC activities can take advantage of Rwanda's increasing emphasis on national pride to promote efforts which convey the message that people must continue to adhere to malaria interventions (LLIN use, IRS, prompt diagnosis, and treatment) to remain successful at keeping malaria at low levels.

Plans and justification

With FY 2014 funding, PMI will continue to support implementation of Rwanda's National Health Communication Strategy, as well as the updated National Malaria Communications Strategy. New plans and strategies for BCC will depend on the success of the activities of the communications project that will begin in FY 2013, which will focus on six high-prevalence districts, and on the changing malaria situation, both in Rwanda and in bordering countries. If the situation evolves as expected, with Rwanda ready for pre-elimination by 2017 in areas with very low prevalence, BCC will focus on risk perception with reminders that malaria can still return, so people should still sleep under nets and be sure to go to the health facility or community health worker if anyone has fever. In districts that share borders with other countries, BCC will need to be intensified for residents, in particular those who cross borders into neighboring countries. Efforts aimed at those who cross borders from countries with strong malaria transmission should be considered as well. These efforts can build on discussion among neighboring countries at the pre-elimination forum regarding possible collaboration activities.

Rwanda has integrated health messaging, which helps extend the reach of malaria-only messages. In addition, the Global Fund has supported and will continue to support a significant amount of malaria BCC efforts. PMI plans to use this funding to target the six high-prevalence districts and evaluate BCC activities' impact.

Proposed activities with FY 2014 funding ($200,000)

- *Community integrated BCC*: PMI, in close collaboration with the NMCP and Rwanda's Health Communications Center, will support community-level efforts to implement promotion of LLINs and case management. Integrated health messaging in interpersonal communication and mass media will be used to promote continued use of LLINs despite declining malaria transmission and prompt malaria diagnosis and treatment. *($200,000)*

Health Systems Strengthening, Capacity Building, and Government-to-Government Transition

NMCP/PMI objectives

Rwanda has devoted significant resources to strengthening its health system, leveraging resources from its national budget, the Global Fund, the USG, and other donors. With these resources, Rwanda has achieved worldwide recognition for its innovative health financing programs, such as performance-based financing and community-based health insurance. These programs, as well as current efforts to determine the costs of essential health services and to pilot a web-based system to track all resources in the health sector are supported by USG and other development partners.

Health systems that allow accessibility to quality affordable health services are critical, as is a strong disease surveillance system to monitor, detect, and respond to disease outbreaks (e.g., malaria and neglected tropical diseases).

Progress during the last 12 months

PMI, as part of broader USG efforts, continued to support capacity building of the national medical store to forecast, procure, store, and distribute health commodities and provided technical assistance to the coordinated procurement and distribution system and the Logistics Management Office for all health commodities. The support included updating the harmonized LMIS nationwide. A team of 30 trainers and six supervisors conducted the updated training reaching 1,850 participants. PMI has also contributed to the requirements gathering for an automated LMIS system.

PMI continued to support human resource needs at the NMCP and quality of laboratory services through the NRL in 2013. PMI supported the development of standard operating procedures and job aids on malaria diagnosis, including external quality control, slide preparation and smear staining. PMI supported a ten-day advanced microscopy training for 11 lab technicians from referral and district hospitals and a five-day training for 31 lab technicians from district hospitals and health centers from the districts of Nyagatare and Kirehe. All 42 district hospitals were supervised at least once in 2012. PMI continued to support the strengthening of M&E systems, including HMIS and community information systems. In particular, PMI supported the linking of the community-based information system SIS-COM to the HMIS.

Capacity Building

The organizational relationships within the Ministry of Health have been restructured with consolidation of many public and private health entities into an overarching center, the Rwandan Biomedical Center. The NMCP sits within the newly approved Rwandan Biomedical Center. The center encompasses malaria, HIV, TB, NRL, and the School of Public Health, and their mandate covers not only all parasitic diseases but also neglected tropical diseases.

Progress during the last 12 months

PMI continued to support three seconded positions (housed at the NMCP):
  1) A logistics officer who started in 2010
  2) An IVM advisor who started in early 2011
  3) An epidemiologist in charge of updating ESR thresholds and responses who started in mid-2011

PMI also supported the Rwandan Field Epidemiology and Laboratory Training Program (FELTP). FELTP is a public health training program to enhance competencies in applied epidemiology, implementation, evaluation, and management of disease interventions, surveillance strengthening, epidemic preparedness and response, and leadership skills. The program is managed and supported by the MoH in collaboration with the School of Public Health, CDC Rwanda, and other partners. FELTP residents have malaria-specific trainings during the course, and the PMI resident advisors have worked with the CDC FELTP advisor to develop and implement malaria-specific projects among malaria FELTP residents including:

  • Develop an insecticide resistance mitigation strategy documenting what additional tests are needed and actions to be taken
  • Pilot an enhanced surveillance/case follow-up in an low prevalence district using CHWs and mobile technology
  • Develop a QA/QC strategy for ensuring quality of RDTs at the community level
  • Implement a therapeutic drug efficacy trial to monitor the effectiveness of ACTs and failure rates
  • Assist in the documentation of best practices and RBM's Progress and Impact Series
  • Conduct a literature search on countries who are in the process of achieving pre-elimination

PMI has supported FELTP malaria residents since FY 2012. Five staff from the NMCP have been part of the FELTP training program to date. During the two-year program, FELTP trainees enroll in a long course in the pursuit of a Masters of Public Health. Following the course portion, the residents take part in a field practicum where they are embedded within the NMCP and work daily with the staff on malaria control issues. Last year, three residents were placed with the malaria branch of the NMCP and have been conducting evaluations of malaria surveillance systems and planned studies on issues related to malaria and malaria diagnostics. To date, five FELTP malaria students have graduated, all of whom have returned to work with the NMCP. The following are presentations and posters from malaria FELTP residents in national and international meetings:

Rukundo, A., Murindahabi, M., Mukabutera A., Karema, C., Binagwaho A. *"Risk factors of underweight among children under five years in Rwanda, 2010"* IP13, 62nd Epidemic Intelligence Service (EIS) Conference, 62 (1), April 22 – 26, 2013, Atlanta, GA.

Umulisa, N., Uwimana A., Karema C., Kabayiza A., Munyaneza, T., Nzayirambaho M. *"Evaluation of Malaria First Response pLDH/HRP2 Combo and SD Bioline Malaria Ag P.f/Pan rapid tests for diagnosis of P. falciparum malaria in June 2011 in Rwanda."* AB007, 1st Rwanda National Field Epidemiology Conference, March 26, 2013, Kigali, Rwanda

Murindahabi M., Rukundo A., Karema C." *Insecticide treated nets (ITNs) usage by under five years children – Rwanda, 2010."* AB008,1[st] Rwanda National Field Epidemiology Conference, March 26, 2013, Kigali, Rwanda

PMI also supports a WHO national program officer who technically supports the NMCP and will help to facilitates cross-border efforts.

Proposed activities with FY 2014 funding ($310,000)

- *Strengthening commodity supply chain management for drugs and other commodities at the central level:* Reinforcing supply chain systems by supporting a logistics officer at the LMO to implement and monitor the new LMIS system for routine quantification, forecasting, and procurement. (Funding included in case management section)

- *Support in-country technical assistance for the implementation of pre-elimination activities:* PMI will support a data manager/epidemiologist as a seconded staff to the NMCP to provide TA on the implementation of pre-elimination activities and surveillance. *($50,000)*

- *Support M&E capacity of the NMCP with supervision, data quality audits, and dissemination:* PMI will support capacity building within the NMCP by supporting supervision visits, quarterly data quality audits, dissemination of best practices, M&E results, and impact at international conferences. *($100,000)*

- *Support to FELTP Program.* PMI will continue to support two malaria residents to the FELTP program and contribute to the advanced training of Rwandan epidemiologists for a 12-month period. The trainees will receive assistance from Resident Advisors and participate in malaria field assignments and investigations throughout Rwanda. *($100,000)*

- *Support WHO National Program Officer for Malaria:* PMI will support a WHO national program officer who will work on promoting cross-border collaboration and finalizing memorandums of understanding which coordinate border malaria control efforts between Rwanda and its malaria endemic neighbors. *($60,000)*

Transition

The GOR has demonstrated not only a strong commitment at the highest levels of government to improving the health of its citizens, but also an ability to manage successfully other direct donor funding from the World Bank, other bilateral donors, and the Global Fund. Given these efforts, over the next five years, a key focus on USG engagement with the GOR is to accelerate support for the sustainable transition of activities to national ownership. Consistent with the intent of the

OECD/DAC 2005 Paris Declaration on Aid Effectiveness, the 2008 Accra Agenda for Action, and the Busan 4th High Level Forum on Aid Effectiveness, PMI will promote host-country ownership, and invest in local capacity development. This transition is closely aligned with Rwanda's GHI Strategy, which integrates key administration priorities, such as PEPFAR, PMI, and Best Practices at Scale in the Home, Community and Facilities.

NMCP/PMI objective

NMCP's and PMI's objective in transitioning to direct government financing for activities is to improve efficiency and save costs in health service delivery.

Progress during the last 12 months

USAID/Rwanda conducted fiduciary risk assessments for different institutions including the Ministry of Health, NMCP, administrative districts, district hospitals, and health centers. Risk mitigation strategies have been developed; however, implementation has been delayed due to lack of guidance, approval, and a possible mechanism. The Mission has received approval to move forward with non-HIV-related transition and will proceed with negotiations of the above risk mitigation strategies with relevant GoR institutions. Also, capacity assessments have been conducted for the transition of both clinical services and IRS, and the respective assessment reports are being finalized. Likewise, this will be followed by negotiations about risk mitigation strategies to address any programmatic weaknesses identified by those assessments. PMI activities will begin to transfer to GOR under the FY 2013 MOP and continue under the FY 2014 MOP, in the amount of $6,180,000 The Mission is working on an overall transition plan, with the goal of signing a transition agreement by October 1^{st,} 2013.

Challenges, opportunities, and threats

Rwanda's strong national commitment and capacity, along with goodwill and support from donors, make government-to-government transitioning of funds a desirable next step in collaborating to prevent and control malaria. Challenges in the areas of capacity and technical assistance will be met with continuing support in those areas.

Plans and justification

PMI, like other USG programs, is planning to provide direct support to GOR to implement some malaria control and prevention activities starting with FY 2013 funds. Originally FY 2012 funds were to be used, but mechanisms for transition were not in place in time. The GOR has demonstrated strong commitment at the highest levels of government to improving the health of its citizens and shown the ability to manage successfully other direct donor funding from the World Bank and Global Fund. Direct financing will help to further build Rwanda's capacity to conduct its own activities and create a more sustainable program.

Proposed activities for FY 2014 for transition through government-to-government ($6,180,000 -funds already included in specific intervention sections)

- *Entomologic monitoring*: Support to conduct entomological monitoring in 12 sentinel sites. *($370,000)*
- *IRS* : Support to the GOR to directly implement IRS, targeting 250,000 structures, and to build capacity to enable decentralization of IRS activities. *($2,500,000)*
- *LLIN study:* Durability monitoring of donated polypropylene nets. *($60,000)*
- *Malaria in pregnancy:*. Training ASM and ANC staff on malaria in pregnancy including early detection and treatment of malaria cases in pregnant women. *($200,000)*
- *Case management:* Strengthening quality assurance and quality control of malaria diagnosis. *($100,000)*
- *Implementation of community case management:* Support implementation of iCCM in 7-10 districts. *($2,000,000)*
- *Monitoring and evaluation*: Enhanced passive surveillance in 5-10 low prevalence districts depending on the cost. This will entail following index cases to their homes in order to obtain individual-based data including geocodes of their residences. *($600,000)*
- *Monitoring and evaluation:* Implementation of health facility survey. ($250,000)
- *Support capacity building of the NMCP for supervision, data quality assurance, and dissemination:* Support to NMCP staff to attend trainings, conferences for capacity building. *($100,000)*

Staffing and Administration

Two health professionals serve as resident advisors to oversee PMI in Rwanda, one representing CDC and one representing USAID. In addition, one or more Foreign Service Nationals work as part of the PMI team. All PMI staff members are part of a single interagency team led by the USAID Mission Director or his/her designee in country. The PMI team shares responsibility for development and implementation of PMI strategies and work plans, coordination with national authorities, managing collaborating agencies and supervising day-today activities. Candidates for resident advisor positions (whether initial hires or replacements) will be evaluated and/or interviewed jointly by USAID and CDC, and both agencies will be involved in hiring decisions, with the final decision made by the individual agency.

The PMI professional staff work together to oversee all technical and administrative aspects of PMI, including finalizing details of the project design, implementing malaria prevention and treatment activities, monitoring and evaluation of outcomes and impact, reporting of results, and providing guidance to PMI partners.

The PMI lead in country is the USAID Mission Director. The two PMI resident advisors, one from USAID and one from CDC, report to the Senior USAID Health Officer for day-to-day leadership, and work together as a part of a single interagency team. The technical expertise housed in Atlanta and Washington guide PMI programmatic efforts and thus overall technical guidance for both RAs falls to the PMI staff in Atlanta and Washington. Since CDC resident advisors are CDC employees (CDC USDD—38), responsibility for completing official performance reviews lies with the CDC Country Director, who is expected to rely upon input from PMI staff across the two agencies that work closely day in and day out with the CDC RA and is thus best positioned to comment on the RA's performance.

The two PMI resident advisors are based within the USAID health office and are expected to spend approximately half their time sitting with and providing technical assistance to the national malaria control programs and partners.

Locally hired staff to support PMI activities either in Ministries or in USAID will be approved by the USAID Mission Director. Because of the need to adhere to specific country policies and USAID accounting regulations, any transfer of PMI funds directly to ministries or host governments will need to be approved by the USAID Mission Director and Controller, in addition to the PMI Coordinator.

($1,137,700)

Table 1: President's Malaria Initiative – Rwanda FY 2014 Budget Breakdown by Partner			
Partner Organization	**Geographic Area**	**Activity**	**Budget ($)**
Pending government-to-government (G2G) mechanism	Nationwide	Entomologic monitoring and evaluation; procure; IRS implementation at 12 sites; net durability and insecticide resistance monitoring; early detection and treatment of malaria in pregnancy; strengthen quality assurance and quality control for malaria diagnosis; iCCM implementation; expand enhanced ESR in 5-10 epidemic-prone districts; implementation of health facility survey; support capacity building of the NMCP for M&E, DQA, and dissemination of country information	6,180,000
TBD	Nationwide	Support supervision by NMCP	150,000
TBD	Targeted districts	IRS implementation	5,034,725
TBD	Nationwide	Technical assistance for net disposal strategy	25,000
TBD	Nationwide	TA to strengthen ESR activities in epidemic-prone districts; conduct readiness assessment for pre-elimination	75,000

TBD	Nationwide	Contribute to DHS 2014-15	100,000
TBD	Nationwide	TA for health facility survey	50,000
TBD	Nationwide	Support decentralized data analysis and response	100,000
TBD	Nationwide	M&E and reporting unit in Mission	100,000
TBD	Nationwide	Support in-country TA for implementation of pre-elimination activities	50,000
Family Health Project	7-10 districts	Technical assistance for iCCM implementation; support Peace Corps	120,000
Society for Family Health	Nationwide	BCC for LLINs, MIP, and CM	200,000
CDC	Targeted districts	IRS technical assistance; develop surveillance system for pre-elimination; support for FELTP trainees	136,300
DELIVER	Nationwide	Procure and distribute 375,000 nets; procurement of CCM commodities; procurement of lab commodities; procurement of malaria drugs; central level supply chain management	4,481,275
USAID/CDC		PMI staff (USAID and CDC) and associated administrative expenses	1,137,700
WHO		Support WHO NPO	60,000
Total			**$18,000,000**

Table 2: President's Malaria Initiative – Rwanda FY 2014 Budget Breakdown by Activity

Planned Obligations for FY 2014

Proposed Activity	Mechanism	Budget Total $	Budget Commodity $	Geographical area	Description
PREVENTIVE ACTIVITIES					
Vector Control - Entomology					
Entomologic monitoring	Pending government to government (G2G) mechanism	370,000		Nationwide	Support for ongoing entomologic monitoring centrally and at 12 sites; support ento technician, equipment, and training at new laboratory
SUBTOTAL VECTOR CONTROL - ENTOMOLOGY		**370,000**	**0**		
Indoor Residual Spraying					
IRS implementation	To be determined (TBD)	5,034,725	4,000,000	Targeted high-prevalence districts, based on HMIS data	Implement spray operations for at least 250,000 structures. Includes procurement of IRS equipment (insecticide, sprayers, PPE etc.), and TA for monitoring and environmental compliance
IRS implementation	Pending G2G mechanism	2,500,000		Targeted high-prevalence districts, based on HMIS data	Implement spray operations including training, implementation, data collection, protocols, guidelines, IEC/BCC, and logistic assessment
IRS technical assistance	CDC	12,100		Targeted high-prevalence districts, based on HMIS data	CDC entomologist technical assistance for monitoring IRS implementation

Activity	Mechanism				
SUBTOTAL IRS		7,546,825	4,000,000		
Insecticide-Treated Nets					
Procure 375,000 nets	DELIVER	2,391,950	2,214,750	Nationwide	Nets to contribute to maintain universal coverage; MPDD management fee (8%)
Distribute 375,000 nets	DELIVER	188,000		Nationwide	Distribution of nets to the community ($0.50 from central warehouse to community through health centers)
Technical assistance for net disposal strategy	TBD	25,000		Nationwide	Provide STTA for long term net disposal strategy
Net durability and insecticide resistance monitoring	Pending G2G mechanism	60,000			Prospective LLIN durability, longevity, and efficacy monitoring of new net products (polypropylene, combination nets)
SUBTOTAL ITNs		2,664,950	2,214,750		
Malaria in Pregnancy (MIP)					
Early detection and treatment of malaria in pregnancy (MIP)	Pending G2G mechanism	200,000	0	Nationwide	Support early detection and treatment of MIP at decentralized levels
SUBTOTAL MIP		200,000	0		
SUBTOTAL PREVENTIVE		10,781,725	6,214,750		
Case Management					
Strengthen quality assurance and quality control for malaria diagnosis	Pending G2G mechanism	100,000	0	Nationwide	Support QA/QC for microscopy and RDTs at HCs and DHs

Activity	Mechanism			Location	Description
Procurement of laboratory commodities	DELIVER	50,000	50,000	Nationwide	Procurement of microscopes and laboratory consumables
Procurement of community case management (CCM) commodities; customs clearance, transport, storage	DELIVER	1,188,000	1,100,000		Procurement of 1,200,000 RDTs for CCM, safety boxes for RDT disposal, and gloves; MPDD management fee (8%)
Procurement, customs clearance, transport, storage of malaria drugs	DELIVER	**363,325**	336,412		Procurement of 350,000 doses of AL and 45,000 vials artesunate and management of AL
Supervision of health facility workers by NMCP	TBD	150,000			Support supervision visits to the district hospitals by the NMCP
Integrated community case management (iCCM)	Pending G2G mechanism	2,000,000	0	7 districts	Implementation of integrated CCM including training and supervision support, tools and registers for CHWs
Technical assistance for implementation of iCCM	Family Health Project	100,000		7 districts	Provide TA for implementation of iCCM nationwide
Support Peace Corps for iCCM	Family Health Project	20,000		7 districts	Support PC/PMI initiative working with iCCM
Central level supply chain management	DELIVER	300,000	0		Support strengthening logistic management information system and coordinated procurement and distribution
SUBTOTAL CASE MANAGEMENT		**4,271,325**	**1,486,412**		

Monitoring and Evaluation (M&E)

Activity	Implementer	Budget		Coverage	Description
Expand enhanced community surveillance, case investigation, and epidemic response in five to ten epidemic-prone districts in the context of pre-elimination	Pending G2G mechanism	600,000	0	5-10 epidemic prone districts	Expand early reporting and case investigation, develop new thresholds and SOPs for ESR, create database for individual reporting, improve HMIS system for transition to pre-elimination
Technical assistance to strengthen ESR activities	TBD	25,000	0	Epidemic prone districts	Support for ESR strategy and system
Develop surveillance system for pre-elimination	CDC	24,200		Nationwide	Assist developing and implementing an enhanced surveillance system with individual case reporting (rather than aggregate case reporting)
Conduct readiness assessment for pre-elimination	TBD	50,000		Nationwide	Assess country's prospects for pre-elimination using Malaria Elimination Group tool
Contribution to DHS 2014-2015	TBD	100,000		Nationwide	Support malaria module and mortality estimates in 2014/2015 DHS
Technical assistance for health facility survey	TBD	50,000		Nationwide	TA for implementation of health facility survey
Implementation of health facility survey 2014	Pending G2G mechanism	250,000		Nationwide	Support implementation of health facility survey
Support decentralized data analysis and response	TBD	100,000		Nationwide	Support building capacity in use of data and response
M&E and reporting unit in Mission	TBD	100,000			Contribute to USAID Mission M&E requirements and responsibilities as they relate to PMI

Activity	Partner	Amount	Location	Description
M&E Total		1,299,200		
Behavior Change Communication (BCC)				
BCC of LLINs, MIP, and CM	Society for Family Health (SFH)	200,000	Nationwide	Community-level support to implement promotion of LLINs and care and repair, repackaging of PRIMO, MIP, and case management
BCC Total		200,000		
Health System Strengthening and Capacity Building				
Support WHO National Program Officer for malaria	WHO	60,000	Nationwide	Support WHO National Program Officer
Support in-country technical assistance for the implementation of pre-elimination activities	TBD	50,000	Nationwide	Support data manager/epidemiologist to provide TA on the implementation of pre-elimination activities and surveillance
Support for FELTP trainees in malaria	CDC	100,000	Nationwide	Support for FELTP trainees in malaria and disease surveillance for capacity building
Support capacity building of the NMCP for M&E, DQA, and dissemination of country information	TBD	100,000	Nationwide	Support NMCP staff to attend trainings and conferences for M&E capacity building and dissemination of success stories
Capacity building Total		310,000		
In-country Staffing and Administration				
PMI staff (USAID and CDC) and associated administrative expenses	USAID/CDC	1,137,700		Support for USAID and CDC Malaria Advisors, Malaria Program Specialist and support staff within USAID Mission plus associated administrative costs.
SUBTOTAL - In-Country Staffing		1,137,700		

GRAND TOTAL		18,000,000		7,701,162		43% commodities